ABRACADABRA

THE STORY of MAGIC
THROUGH THE AGES

ABRACADABRA

THE STORY OF MAGIC
THROUGH THE AGES

HP NEWQUIST

with illustrations by OLGA & ALEKSEY IVANOV

SQUARE
FISH

HENRY HOLT AND COMPANY
NEW YORK

SQUARE
FISH

An imprint of Macmillan Publishing Group, LLC
175 Fifth Avenue, New York, NY 10010
mackids.com

ABRACADABRA: THE STORY OF MAGIC THROUGH THE AGES. Text copyright © 2015
by HP Newquist. Illustrations copyright © 2015 by Olga & Aleksey Ivanov.
All rights reserved. Printed in the United States of America by LSC Communications,
Harrisonburg, Virginia.

Square Fish and the Square Fish logo are trademarks of Macmillan and
are used by Henry Holt and Company under license from Macmillan.

Our books may be purchased in bulk for promotional, educational, or business use. Please
contact your local bookseller or the Macmillan Corporate and Premium Sales Department at
(800) 221-7945 ext. 5442 or by e-mail at MacmillanSpecialMarkets@macmillan.com.

Permission to use the following images is gratefully acknowledged:
Francis George: 121; HP Newquist: 21; Library of Congress: 25, 54, 59, 64, 69, 70,
72, 73, 74, 75, 78, 82, 87, 88, 92, 109, 110, 123; WG Alma Conjuring Collection,
State Library Victoria: 100; Wikimedia: 13, 27, 33, 34, 113

Library of Congress Cataloging-in-Publication Data
Newquist, H. P. (Harvey P.)
Abracadabra : the story of magic through the ages / HP Newquist ;
with illustrations by Aleksey & Olga Ivanov.
pages   cm
ISBN 978-1-250-11539-3 (paperback)   ISBN 978-1-62779-525-8 (ebook)
1. Magic tricks—History—Juvenile literature.   2. Magic—History—Juvenile literature.
I. Ivanov, A. (Aleksey), ill.   II. Ivanov, O. (Olga), ill.   III. Title.
GV1548.N48 2015   793.8—dc23   2015000406

Originally published in the United States by Henry Holt and Company
First Square Fish Edition: 2017
Book designed by Meredith Pratt
Square Fish logo designed by Filomena Tuosto

1   3   5   7   9   10   8   6   4   2

AR: 7.3

TO MY FRIENDS...
and you know who you are.

*Because having good friends is
an extraordinarily magical thing.*

CONTENTS

INTRODUCTION

MAGIC IS A WORD THAT HAS BEEN USED THROUGHOUT history. People used it for centuries to describe things they saw but didn't understand. Magic was the explanation for earthquakes and insect plagues and floods. Even as mankind moved into modern times, people who saw engines and telephones and radios and electrical appliances for the first time thought they were seeing magic at work.

Today magic still describes things we see yet cannot understand. Now, however, it applies to entertainment. Magicians are able to perform tricks that cause us to doubt what we think is possible and what is not. They can do this by having us pick a card—any card—and telling us what it is . . . even while they're blindfolded. Or they can put on a huge stage show complete with animals, lights, characters, smoke, mirrors, and loud music . . . and make people disappear right in front of our eyes.

Magic is deception. Good magic fools us so completely that we don't feel like we have been tricked or deceived. Instead we feel like we have seen the impossible—seen something that we cannot explain, something amazing.

Magicians have no special powers. They are not wizards or gods or supernatural beings or aliens. Magicians are people with very specific skills—just as doctors have skills, and acrobats have skills. The magician's skills allow him or her to do things most of us cannot do. A magician can saw a human being in half and then put the two pieces back together. A magician can tear up our favorite photograph, throw it in the garbage, and then pull that same photo out of an envelope in their pocket—in perfect condition. A magician can be handcuffed and chained inside a tank of water and escape in the time it takes to count to three.

Believe it or not, there are only a few types of magic. Most magic falls into one of five categories. Within those categories, though, there are hundreds, even thousands, of tricks.

The first category of magic is called Sleight of Hand. It is also known as prestidigitation, which means the "quick movement of fingers." In Sleight of Hand, a magician uses their fingers and hands to make everyday objects disappear, change position, or transform from one thing into another. These objects can be coins, cards, handkerchiefs, scarves, keys, watches, cell phones, or any other small item that can fit into the hand.

The second category is called Conjuring. This is when a magician makes something appear out of nowhere, such as pulling a rabbit out of a hat or making a person appear from an empty box. Conjurers can also make any number of things disappear, and over the years this has included everything from elephants to airplanes.

The third category is Illusion. This is one of the most complicated forms of magic. Illusion involves making an audience believe it is seeing something other than what is actually happening. It usually takes place on a stage and involves special equipment. Sawing a person in half, floating in the air, and walking on water are all forms of Illusion.

A fourth category of magic is Escaping. Called Escapology, it involves magicians getting out of seemingly inescapable—and oftentimes dangerous—situations. These situations range from being tied to a chair or locked in handcuffs to being encased in a sealed tank of water or chained inside a cage.

Finally there is Mentalism, also known as Mind Reading. Mentalists are the magicians who seem able to predict the future or guess what people are thinking or tell people secret things about themselves that no one else knows.

Good magicians are masters at encouraging a suspension of disbelief. This means you start out disbelieving something is possible, but you are persuaded to change your mind, and possibly start believing after all. If I told you that I could saw someone in half, you wouldn't believe it. But if I *showed* you I could do it as part of a magic act, you'd probably change your mind. You'd put aside—or suspend—your disbelief.

The best magicians do more than get us to suspend our disbelief. They leave us shaking our heads and wondering, *How did they do that?* In most cases, we'll never know how they did it. But as you'll find in the pages to come, sometimes you will get the answers.

ABRACADABRA

THE STORY OF MAGIC THROUGH THE AGES

CHAPTER ONE

THE MYTHICAL ORIGINS OF MAGIC

MAGICIANS WEREN'T BORN WITH THE KNOWLEDGE OF HOW to perform magic. Someone had to teach them how to do their tricks. And before that, someone had to create the tricks. After all, magic tricks and illusions didn't just appear out of thin air. Someone had to figure out what they wanted a trick to be, then how to perform it, and then make it so amazing that it would fool everyone.

So who came up with these magic tricks?

For the answer to that, we have to go back through history. We have to go back a few thousand years, because it turns out that people have been doing magic for a very, very long time.

There is one magic trick that has been performed more than any other in history. This trick is performed by all kinds of magicians, whether they are on a big Las Vegas stage or sitting at a small table on a city sidewalk. Called Cups and Balls, it is a very simple sleight of hand trick. The magician hides balls under cups, then moves the cups around on a tabletop. When he lifts the cups, the balls have magically switched places or disappeared.

Some magicians believe that Cups and Balls is the oldest magic trick in the world. They claim there is evidence of it being per-formed in ancient Egypt. They point to a cemetery called Beni Hasan, located along the banks of the Nile River. The cemetery contains thirty-nine tombs—many of which are four thousand years old—carved out of the rock hills. The cemetery is historically important because the walls of the tombs were painted with scenes of ancient Egyptian life and contain numerous ancient picture symbols called hieroglyphs.

The tombs of Beni Hasan

Cups and Balls

What makes the Beni Hasan cemetery important to our story is that there is one scene painted on a wall that shows two people facing each other. The people appear to be moving cups in the same way that modern magicians do with Cups and Balls. While no one knows for sure, many magicians believe that this painting shows Egyptians performing Cups and Balls—more than forty centuries ago.

Ancient Egypt is home to many mysteries and legends, from the Sphinx and the building of the pyramids to the stories of King Tut and Cleopatra. But some of its most incredible legends were about magic and about men who may have been the first magicians. These stories were depicted in hieroglyphs on an Egyptian document known as the Westcar Papyrus, which was written more than three thousand years ago. In one story, an advisor to the Egyptian pharaoh makes a crocodile out of wax. When he throws the wax crocodile into the water, it magically comes alive as a real crocodile.

In another story, the pharaoh's daughter is riding in a boat. During the ride, she accidentally loses a piece of turquoise jewelry when it falls into the water. Her guardians and assistants spend hours looking for it, but no one can find the precious stone. Then another of the pharaoh's advisors shows up to help. This man does something unheard of: he folds the water in half. The turquoise can be seen at the bottom of the river, and it is recovered. The advisor then folds the water back into place.

The most intriguing story of magic from the Westcar Papyrus is about Dedi, a man living quietly in a small Egyptian village. Dedi is said to be 110 years old. He has a huge appetite, eating five hundred loaves of bread and two hundred pounds of meat a day.

The Westcar Papyrus told stories of ancient magicians.

What makes him even more unusual, though, is that he has the power to remove and reattach the heads of animals without killing them.

When the pharaoh, named Khufu, hears of this, he summons Dedi to his palace. On the day Dedi arrives, Khufu asks that a criminal be brought to the palace from a local jail. He wants Dedi to cut off the prisoner's head and then reattach it. But Dedi refuses Khufu's request, saying that such things should not be done to people.

The pharaoh agrees and comes up with a different idea. He orders that a duck be brought to the palace, then a goose, then an ox. Each of the animals is decapitated, one after another, and Dedi speaks magic words over them. Suddenly their heads are reattached to their necks . . . and they come back to life and are perfectly normal. The duck and goose flutter out of the palace while the ox slowly walks away. Amazed by Dedi's powers, Khufu invites Dedi to come live in the palace. From then on, Dedi is fed a thousand loaves of bread and an entire ox every day.

Many other ancient cultures also had stories about men (and sometimes women) who did things that no one else could do. Ancient Greece had people called oracles—a sort of holy magician—who could predict the future. Priests

Oracles predicted the future.

in the Aztec and Incan civilizations of South America had powers that allowed them to talk to their gods. Many of these legendary magicians were believed to control the sun, the weather, and even life and death.

The most famous of these men was a magician named Merlin. His legend and popularity over the centuries has been so great that Merlin has served as the inspiration for every long-bearded wizard and trusted advisor you've ever heard of, from Gandalf in *The Lord of the Rings* to Harry Potter's mentor, Albus Dumbledore.

Merlin was said to have lived in the sixth century, when he helped the young King Arthur rule over Britain (what is now England, Scotland, and Wales). Merlin served as Arthur's teacher and guided

Merlin, the model for today's wizards

the king on his many adventures. Stories about the wizard said that his mother was human and his father was a spirit, which was why Merlin could perform magic and create illusions. He could change his shape, protect Arthur with spells, and see into the future. He is even credited with creating the famous Stonehenge rock formation in England by moving its monstrously huge stones all the way from Ireland—which is hundreds of miles away, over the waters of the Irish Sea.

The problem with these astounding stories is that no one is quite certain whether King Arthur, let alone his trusty aide Merlin, ever really existed. There are no documents from that time to prove they were actual people.

True or not, Merlin has been the model for many magicians in literature and in the movies for more than a thousand years. Like Merlin, these wizards and sorcerers were able to cast spells, create potions, and change people into animals and animals into people. They wore pointed hats and long robes decorated with stars and moons. And it was often their job to protect a young prince or a king or a youngster on a quest. Wizards like Merlin practiced only good magic, also known as white magic.

On the opposite side of the mystical world from good wizards were witches and warlocks, who practiced bad or black magic. These magicians were said to get their powers from evil spirits, and they used this magic to harm their enemies or make themselves more powerful. They preferred to do their work at night, when their evil deeds and meetings with demons would be hidden by darkness.

The fear of black magic was rampant during a period of history known as the Dark Ages. During the Dark Ages, from about the fifth century to the twelfth century, much of Europe was in ruins. Entire countries had been destroyed by wars, disease, plagues, and famine. Many regions of the continent had no laws or governments. Schools had all but vanished, and living conditions

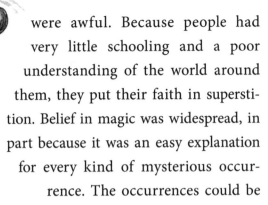

were awful. Because people had very little schooling and a poor understanding of the world around them, they put their faith in superstition. Belief in magic was widespread, in part because it was an easy explanation for every kind of mysterious occurrence. The occurrences could be anything from a natural event such as an earthquake to the ability of a man to make a coin disappear. Even simple juggling was considered a form of magic.

At this time, Europeans believed that good things came from God and bad things came from the devil. Many churches in Europe even claimed that magicians were friends of the devil. Surely, the churches stated, no one could make objects vanish by uttering a few words and waving their hands. Even priests, who were supposed to be able to communicate directly with God, could not do this. Since God didn't give men and women magical powers, there was only one explanation for magicians: they must have gotten their special powers from the devil. The thinking was that magicians probably had to sell their souls to the devil in return for being able to create magic.

Because fear and superstition were rampant in the Dark Ages, anyone who acted strangely or looked different was often suspected of practicing black magic. Witch hunts occurred regularly throughout Europe as villagers sought to destroy anyone they thought might be a witch. Many suspected witches were arrested and executed. No proof of their guilt was needed. If a man didn't like a woman in his neighborhood, he might accuse her of flying through the air or claim she had turned him into a newt. The accusation alone was enough to have the woman thrown in jail.

One of the first magicians to be accused of associating with the devil was a man named Triscalinus. While performing for King Charles IX of France in the mid-1500s, Triscalinus made

King Charles IX with Triscalinus

rings disappear from the fingers of one of the king's attendants. The rings magically reappeared in Triscalinus's hands, even though he was on the other side of the room. In a fit of horror, the audience grabbed the magician. They threatened to kill him if he did not confess that the devil had helped him with the trick. To save his life, so the story goes, Triscalinus confessed.

On a smaller scale there were real crooks who used the simplest type of magic—Sleight of Hand—to rob unsuspecting townspeople. Not surprisingly, the Cups and Balls Trick showed up in the hands of these criminals. A painting by Dutch artist Hieronymus Bosch from around 1500 called *The Conjurer* depicts an event that involves both magic and stealing. In some translations this painting is called *The Magician*. A magician is shown at a table with cups and balls in front of him. He has just caused a small frog to appear from the mouth of a man in the audience, and another frog sits quietly on the table. He is obviously a magician who is good at what he does.

On closer examination, though, the painting is not about the magician's tricks. In the back of the audience is another man who looks like he is not very interested in what is going on. That is because he is taking the coin purse from an old man's belt. The pickpocket and the magician are likely working together, and the magic show is a way to distract people so their valuables can be stolen.

In addition to being called friends of the devil, now magicians were also called cheats, liars, and thieves. Their reputation had gotten so bad that magicians were regularly thrown in jail and, in some cases, even executed.

The Conjurer (The Magician), *by Hieronymous Bosch*

ABRACADABRA

Abracadabra is a word with no meaning, but it has been used as a magic word for centuries. No one is sure where the word originated, but we know it was used as far back as the second century. That was when a man named Quintus Serenus Sammonicus wrote a medical book stating that the word *abracadabra* had magical powers and could cure diseases.

Abracadabra could not just be shouted out at random, though. For the word to work, it had to be written repeatedly in a triangular pattern on a piece of paper or cloth, with each line of the word having one fewer letter than the one above it. At the bottom, the only remaining letter would be an *A*. This writing had to be worn around the patient's neck for nine days, after which it was supposed to be tossed into a river. Only then would the sufferer be cured.

Part of the belief in *abracadabra* came from the fact that it diminished to nothing when written as prescribed . . . which was also what was supposed to happen to the disease. This may have inspired early magicians to use the word when they made something disappear during a performance. Shouting a magical word just as a trick was revealed was a way to add flair to the moment. *Abracadabra*, being a nonsense word, worked perfectly. It had a long, albeit ineffective, history of being used as a magical cure, yet it wasn't a common word or phrase like *Look!* or *See here!* or *Get ready for this!* It was also a word that was pleasing to the ear—caused by all the short *a* sounds—and long enough that magicians could say it for several seconds to drag out the tension of a trick. It could also be made to sound either mysterious or playful—depending on what effect the magician wanted the trick to have on his audience.

Today *abracadabra* is used by magicians all over the world, but the word has also entered common use. People say it to reference doing something seemingly impossible. For example: *So you're just going to—abracadabra—fly to Mars?* or *I can spend ten minutes online and—abracadabra—I'll be able to speak fluent Mandarin.*

No matter how it's used, *abracadabra* has a magical quality. It will always be the most important word in a magician's bag of tricks.

A B R A C A D A B R A
A B R A C A D A B R
A B R A C A D A B
A B R A C A D A
A B R A C A D
A B R A C A
A B R A C
A B R A
A B R
A B
A

CUPS AND BALLS

The audience thinks the three balls pass through the three solid cups. The key to the trick is that there are actually four balls.

HERE'S HOW TO PERFORM IT.

Start with three stackable cups, like plastic or paper cups. Make sure they're not clear, or the trick won't work. It also helps if they're white on the inside. Next, take four small squishy balls—or if you don't have them, take a napkin and tear it into four equal parts, and crumple each part into a tiny ball.

Line the three cups right side up on a table, with one ball sitting in front of each cup. While you're setting this up, slip the fourth ball into the middle cup. You can also do this earlier; just don't let

anyone see the ball inside the cup. Also, try to keep some distance between you and the audience so it can't get too close or see over the top of the cups.

Now flip all the cups upside down. If you do it fast enough, the ball will stay in the middle cup and not drop out. It will be hidden under the middle cup and no one will know.

Place the ball that's sitting in front of the middle cup on top of it (on the bottom of the cup). Then stack the other cups, one after another, on top of the middle cup. The ball you placed on top of the cup is now sandwiched between the first and second cups.

Lift the whole stack up. The ball you hid in the middle cup will now be revealed, making it appear that the ball you just placed on top of the cup somehow passed right through it. (Remember, the audience didn't know that the ball was already underneath the middle cup.)

Now that you've done this, tilt the stack in your hand so it's facing upward (open side toward the ceiling), and pull them apart to place them back in a row upside down. Make sure the second cup goes over the ball that was just revealed. What happens is that the ball you placed on the top of the cup earlier is now in the second cup, and by tipping it over the first ball, you've now got two balls under the cup. Again, the audience doesn't know this.

Repeat this process, and add another ball on the middle cup. Stack the cups again, lift them up, and reveal two balls.

Do it again, and then all three balls end up under the cups. Pull the cups apart, but don't let anyone see that the fourth ball still sits inside the second cup.

ᴬᴺᴰ ABRACADABRA—

there you have it.
You have just performed the
oldest magic trick in history.

CHAPTER TWO

FTER SUFFERING THROUGH HUNDREDS OF YEARS OF THE
Dark Ages, European nations began to reestablish themselves in the 1500s. People began to look to both science and
religion instead of local superstition to help them understand their
daily lives. Many felt that science could explain the mysteries of
the natural world. They believed humans should study the sun
and stars, the animal and plant world, and even the human body,
to figure out how things really worked. These early scientists
realized that what had been labeled as magic could be explained
through reason and methodical observation. They started exploring chemistry, physics, anatomy, and astronomy.

Nonetheless, religion was still a more important part of people's
lives than science. And many religious leaders of the time didn't
like science, believing that scientists were trying to ruin religion
and take away the role of priests in society. To stop scientists and
others who didn't follow its teachings, the church began inquisitions. These inquisitions were periods of time when the pope and
his priests ordered that anyone who did not practice religion the

way that the church demanded should be imprisoned, tortured, or executed.

While inquisitions spread throughout Europe, England continued its witch hunts. People were accused of practicing magic and were then convicted of befriending and worshipping the devil.

In 1584 a man named Reginald Scot published a book called *The Discoverie of Witchcraft*. Scot was appalled by witch hunts and angry that innocent people who practiced magic were thrown in jail or executed. Scot knew they were being persecuted wrongly because he understood that magic was based on nothing more than tricks. In his book he stated that there were no such things as

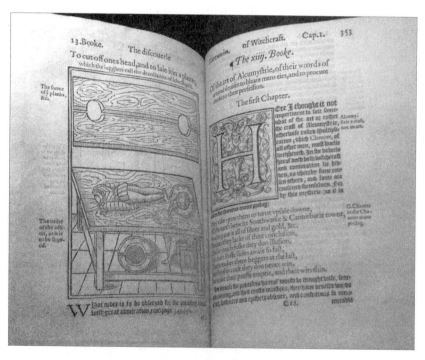

The Discoverie of Witchcraft

witches or wizards, and no one on Earth had the power to control nature or change the things God had made.

Scot argued that the ability to create illusions or perform sleight of hand tricks was nothing more than an entertaining skill—and everyone could benefit from a little entertainment. To prove witches didn't have mysterious powers, Scot explained how many magical tricks were performed. He described in great detail some of the more impressive feats of the time, like swallowing knives and passing coins through solid objects. He even included an illustration to show how the decapitation trick—made famous by Dedi—worked. His hope was, if people understood that magic was harmless fun, the witch hunts would stop.

By stating that witches and magicians were simply good performers—who did occasionally break the law by cheating their audiences—Scot angered England's religious and government leaders, men who actually did believe in witches. King James I was especially upset; he seemed to think that there were witches everywhere, and he wanted them killed. Scot's book made the king's pursuit of witches look silly. Outraged, King James and his soldiers gathered up every copy of *The Discoverie of Witchcraft* they could find. Then they burned them. The witch hunts continued.

Fortunately, a few of Scot's books survived the fires. Nearly a hundred years later, after King James had died, bookmakers printed new versions of *The Discoverie of Witchcraft*. These copies, with their descriptions of how tricks were performed, were purchased by a curious generation of would-be magicians in the late 1600s. Because witch hunts were over by that time—with a few exceptions—the art of performing magic gained newfound popularity. People throughout Europe, and especially in Britain, began to re-create the tricks that only a hundred years earlier might have gotten those people burned at the stake.

Other magic books were soon published, many of them using Scot's descriptions of the secrets behind the tricks. Magicians started appearing at public gatherings and festivals, in town squares and on street corners. Crowds welcomed the magicians, and even cheered them on. Their tricks were entertaining, not threatening. No one confused these performers with witches.

Gradually, more people realized science could explain things that had long been mysterious. They began to doubt that magicians controlled the powers of nature or were friends of the devil. They came to believe science could help them understand the world. In fact, for a while, early scientists were the new magicians.

These magician-scientists were called alchemists. Unlike modern scientists, who seek to find answers to why nature works the way it does, alchemists were concerned with the opposite: explaining nature and then changing the way it worked. Many of them tried to turn ordinary metals like lead into gold, something that would make them—and the people they worked for—rich beyond belief. Alchemists also concocted potions they hoped would allow them to live forever, or at least stay young for a very long time.

As alchemists attempted to achieve these goals—all the while entertaining kings and queens with their bubbling potions and smoky spectacles—they conducted hundreds and thousands of scientific experiments. They knew they had to understand the way the world worked in order to change it. But they had much to learn.

For instance, alchemists didn't know that gold and lead were made from different atoms, so there was no way to turn one into the other. Such knowledge would have saved them the time and trouble of trying to do the impossible.

Yet in the process of their experiments—and often by accident—these early scientists began to unravel the secrets of nature. They learned a great deal about chemistry, chemical reactions, and how different substances worked together. This led to huge advances in the manufacture of porcelain, metal, and glass. Their notes and experiments established a foundation for future generations of scientists. Just as important, the alchemists proved that the world was not such a mysterious place after all.

By the 1700s, the idea of being able to control nature with magic was almost completely gone. There were still places—including America—where people believed in witches, but advances in science had taken the fear factor out of magic. In an age of science and reason, people knew that magic was not real.

Magic continued to be popular, but it had not changed significantly in hundreds of years. The tricks were the same ones that had been around since the time of the ancient Egyptians. The setting wasn't much improved either, with the exception of the few magicians lucky enough to perform in grand castle halls and stages for kings and queens.

The tricks remained small no matter where people saw them. Because magicians generally performed outdoors and traveled from town to town, many relied on sleight of hand tricks and others that could be performed with very little preparation and just a few common objects. Cups and Balls was a regular part

*An alchemist working in his laboratory
with an assistant*

of their acts, as were card tricks, sword swallowing, fire eating, and making small animals appear and disappear. The magicians would set up quickly, perform for an audience, hope to collect a few coins from onlookers, and then move on. They were street performers much like those who can be found in every big city today.

As an art form, magic was not impressive. People would just as soon stop on the street to see a musical group or an acrobat as they would a magician. Magic on the street lacked a sense of majesty and mystery. If someone wanted majesty and mystery—in other words, a big show—they went to the theater or the opera.

It took someone quite unusual to begin the process of making magic into a big show. That someone was a man named Matthias Buchinger. And he was about as unusual a man as has ever lived.

Buchinger was born in Germany on June 3, 1674. It seemed unlikely that he would ever be a famous magician. He was born with no hands and no legs. As an adult, he was only twenty-nine inches tall.

Yet Buchinger learned how to paint and write using the ends of his arms. He also became a master craftsman, building musical instruments that he taught himself how to play. But he was most famous for being able to perform magic. He was a master of Cups and Balls, card tricks, and making birds appear seemingly out of nowhere.

His skill as an artist, a musician, and a magician made him popular with royal families and audiences throughout Europe in the early 1700s. Buchinger performed in Germany for many years before traveling to England, where he amazed Britain's King

A portrait of Matthias Buchinger

George. He then went to Ireland, and liked it so much, he decided to live there. He performed stage shows regularly in cities around Ireland, attracting large crowds who stared in disbelief at how talented this tiny man was.

Buchinger's physical challenges and travel schedule did not keep him from having an intriguing personal life. He was married at least three times and may have had as many as fifteen children.

His ability to perform tricks that most people with all their fingers could never do won Buchinger praise across the European continent. His shows were held on stages, and people paid money to see him perform. His tricks, although not much different from those performed by other magicians, were all the more impressive because of his handicap and his amazing skill. Buchinger's unusual appearance certainly had much to do with his popularity, but the fact that he is remembered for his magical prowess shows how talented he was as a performer. He had proved magic could be a big show that could attract big crowds, and he became famous for establishing the stage as a new venue for magicians.

By the mid-1700s magicians found themselves competing with scientists for attention. Science was new to people, and it was almost as mysterious as magic. Microscopes revealed that the world was made of unseen organisms. Chemistry showed how different elements in nature formed everything from water to

blood. Astronomy proved that there were other planets beyond our own and that those planets circled the sun. Physics demonstrated the forces that resulted in floods and volcanoes. It was an exciting time of discovery.

Public science demonstrations, such as chemical reactions that resulted in flashes of bright colors and smoke, or projectors that showed skin cells under a microscope, were popular with audiences. People were amazed at the variety of things scientists were discovering, and they loved seeing them.

Yet science and magic seem to be the complete opposites of each other. Science is all about uncovering mysteries and explaining how the universe works. Magic is about keeping secrets and making people believe in things that aren't real.

Once scientists were able to explain many of the workings of the natural world, and people understood how some magic tricks worked, it was harder to fool people than it had been in the past. For instance, everyone knew that a person wrapped in heavy chains and locked in a water tank could not survive. Everyone knew that a man could not catch a speeding bullet with his teeth or swallow an entire sword. Everyone knew that a man couldn't take the head off a bird and then reattach it to make the bird just like new.

Everyone knew these things were impossible, so magicians had to work harder than ever to make people believe that such things could be done. And that was when magic became really interesting.

NEARLY EVERYONE interested in magic begins with sleight of hand tricks. Even the famous magician Houdini started by doing sleight of hand tricks, which were popular in sideshows. These were simple illusions or card and coin tricks. A very easy one is levitating a simple object like a fork. Take a fork and hold it in your right fist, making sure to hold it vertically. Have your clenched fingers face away from the audience so it is seeing the back of your hand. Grab your right hand with your left hand, around the wrist. Wrap your left-hand fingers and thumb around your right wrist—except for your left index finger. Slide that into your closed right fist so it holds the fork against your palm.

It should look like this:

Now open your right fist slowly, giving the fork a bit of a wiggle with the index finger of your left hand.

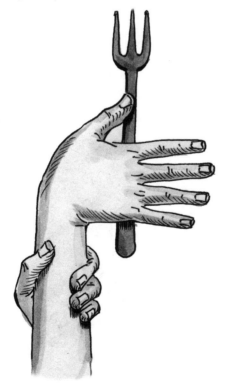

When your fist is completely uncurled, it will look like the fork is floating on its own. This trick is aided by a great show of struggling or trying to force "power" from one hand to another. It is important to remember that a good magician doesn't just know how to do the trick; a good magician knows how to perform it so well that the audience believes it.

SCIENCE SHOWS *and* MAGICAL MARVELS

THE POPULARITY OF SCIENCE PRESENTATIONS CONVINCED magicians they should incorporate some of science's theatrical and dramatic elements into their own acts. Magicians began studying the science shows to get ideas about how to make their own performances more entertaining.

One popular component of early science shows was mechanical figures that seemed to come alive. Called automata

(awe-TAH-muh-tah), they were constructed with metal gears and springs and were crafted to resemble living creatures. They were often used in clock towers, where they came out and danced and played musical instruments at certain hours during the day. Automata operated without any obvious help from strings or other external forces, and their inner workings were always carefully hidden.

An early example was created by Albertus Magnus, a German bishop and philosopher born around 1200 CE. Magnus is said to have spent nearly thirty years of his life building a mechanical head that could think for itself. The head, which was made of brass, was able to answer questions that were put to it and was capable of solving mathematical problems. Eventually, according to legend, Magnus was able to affix a body to the head, creating a walking robot very similar to C-3PO from *Star Wars*.

Some artists made automata that stood alone and behaved just like humans and animals. In the 1730s a French craftsman named Jacques de Vaucanson built a mechanical flute player that could play a dozen tunes

Jacques de Vaucanson, who built lifelike automata

on a real flute. It was an intricate piece of machinery, yet all it could do was play the flute. De Vaucanson became more famous for building a mechanical duck that he exhibited all over Europe. This automaton (the singular of automata) contained more than four thousand parts and was able to walk and flap its wings. It could

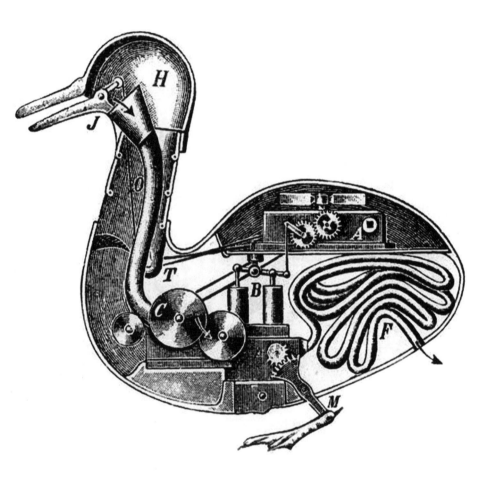

The hidden workings of Vaucanson's duck

even eat exactly like a real, live duck. The duck could grab the grain with its bill, swallow it, and then excrete the result. De Vaucanson did this by building a complex set of gears, tubing, and various secret mechanisms inside the duck. Throughout his life, he refused to show anyone how the duck worked.

One of the most imaginative automata was constructed by Pierre Jacquet-Droz in the late 1700s. Called *The Writer*, it was a mechanical boy made of approximately six thousand parts. The mechanical boy sat at a table and held a pen and, on command, could write selected poems on a piece of paper. Other automata around Europe could play chess or tell fortunes or smoke pipes or answer questions.

Automata appeared to be magical creatures. If you opened them up, though, you would see the pumps and the fluids and the moving parts that made them work. The springs, gears, tubing, and other mechanical devices inside the automata would eventually inspire magicians to use the same technology to create a new kind of stage act.

The man who brought science and magic together, in part by using automata, was an Italian science professor named Giuseppe Pinetti. Born in 1750, Pinetti was so good at demonstrating chemistry and physics in his classroom that even people who weren't his students would ask to see his science demonstrations. Realizing he had a gift for educating and entertaining, Pinetti decided to perform his science experiments in public.

Pinetti also used a few sleight of hand tricks as part of his science lectures, knowing that they would attract curious audiences. Calling himself Professor Pinetti, he wanted to set himself apart from other magicians. Common magicians did tricks, waited for applause, and collected money. As far as he was concerned, that was boring. Instead Professor Pinetti was determined to make his shows something grand, something people would talk about long after they had left the theater.

He began by dressing as if he were a nobleman, wearing very expensive clothing. He then built a stage in a Paris theater that featured elegant decorations to make it feel like he and the audience were in a palace. Chandeliers and fine furniture made his stage seem luxurious. Unbeknownst to the audience, these decorations were also part of the act; they helped conceal some of the tools he used to perform his tricks. Pinetti's style of magic was so extravagant that it *had* to be performed on a specially designed indoor stage. This was not a show that could be done on a table or a sidewalk. It featured machinery, magic cabinets, lengths of rope, and specially designed equipment. Plus, Pinetti had all kinds of tools and objects that helped make his shows something no street performer could ever do. These

Professor Giuseppe Pinetti

Pinetti onstage

items came to be known as *props* because they were part of the property that the magician set out on the stage.

The Professor also changed the way magicians behaved onstage. He acted as if he were the most important, most mysterious, and most intelligent person in the room. Instead of being a mere performer, there only to amuse, he positioned himself as an authority—someone to be listened to and watched carefully. He took charge of the stage as if he were conducting an orchestra or presenting an extraordinary classroom lesson. As a result, Pinetti's audience always paid attention to him.

In 1784 Pinetti's fame became so widespread that he traveled to London to perform in a theater usually reserved for plays. He charged an admission fee that was as much as a theater ticket, which was considered an extravagant sum to most people. This may have been the first time a magician presented his act in a truly respectable place (or at least what the richest and most powerful people in London thought was respectable). Pinetti's show, like opera and ballet, was proper entertainment, not just something that scoundrels performed at festivals and street fairs.

Reports from papers of the time indicate that the Professor was good at his tricks, but not great (like Buchinger). However, he did have one trick that made him especially famous, something that other magicians couldn't do. And the reason they couldn't do it was because they didn't have the elaborate equipment Pinetti had.

To begin his famous trick, the Professor brought onstage a tiny orange tree in a pot. He watered it with what he claimed was a magical liquid. Suddenly, and quite quickly, the tree started growing, and full-size oranges appeared on its branches. The tiny plant had blossomed into a mature fruit tree in just a few seconds. Pinetti then plucked oranges from the tree and gave them to the audience to eat.

It was a remarkable trick that wowed audiences hundreds of years ago . . . and it is popular to this day. (The trick is in knowing that it wasn't a real orange tree, and that automata don't always have to be in the shape of humans or animals. Sometimes mechanical marvels can be in the shape of trees.)

Pinetti's act was a turning point in magic. His glamorous stage setup and his commanding presence impressed audiences, and they always left wanting to see more. He was applauded every time he took the stage, and people paid him a lot of money to perform. In a way, the Professor was like magic's first rock star. As soon as other magicians saw how much audiences enjoyed seeing magic in a wondrous setting, they copied Pinetti's stage setup and his showmanship.

An inside look at Pinetti's orange tree

TOOLS OF THE TRADE: SMOKE

When magicians first made their way to the stage in enclosed buildings, they were aided by something perhaps not entirely expected: smoke and darkness. Performed on street corners during the day, magicians' tricks were limited by how much the audience could see in the sunlight. Magicians couldn't allow the audience to see them pulling things out from under a table or out of a sleeve—things that were easy to see in broad daylight. They also couldn't perform outside at night because then the audience couldn't see anything at all, which was just as bad.

Being indoors for magicians was like opening a whole new bag of tricks. First of all, magicians could light just the part of the stage they wanted the audience to see. Putting a bright spotlight on a table covered in white cloth or on a woman in a bright white dress made the rest of the stage seem much darker. This darkness and the glare of the white cloth helped to conceal thin black wires and machinery painted with flat dull black paint. By shifting where spotlights were at a particular time, the magician could focus the audience's eyes exactly where he wanted them. The rest of the stage would be hidden in shadows.

In the early days of magic theater, spotlights were not the electrical lights we see in theaters and concert halls today. They were like high-intensity candles. They created a bright light by burning a chalky white chemical known as lime. (Even today, we say that celebrities are "living in the limelight.") These limelights gave off a white hazy smoke, which floated about the stage. Additionally, the rest of the theater was dimly lit by gaslight, which produced a bit of its own smoke.

Early stage magic was performed at a time when people regularly smoked cigarettes, cigars, and pipes wherever they went. When this smoke was added to the gaslights and the limelights in the theater, it created another layer of haze—like a very light fog—that hung in the air around the stage. This haze further helped the magician keep some of his secrets away from the prying eyes of the audience.

Eventually the use of electric lights and a general ban on indoor cigarette smoking eliminated this smoke screen from the magician's bag of tricks. To make up for this, performers today use high-tech smoke and fog machines to create the haze that helps cover up parts of the trick.

In 1805, five years after the death of Professor Pinetti, the first spectacular stage magician was born. He was a Frenchman named Jean Robert-Houdin, and he would one day be known as the father of modern magic.

Robert-Houdin began his career as a maker of watches and clocks. In addition to timepieces, he built his own automata, including little robotlike people that performed circus acts. One of these automata was purchased by P. T. Barnum, whose name would eventually be associated with the biggest circus in the world, the Ringling Bros. and Barnum & Bailey Circus.

One day, Robert-Houdin went to a bookshop to buy two books on advanced clockmaking. The bookseller wasn't paying attention and accidentally gave him two books on how to perform magic tricks. Robert-Houdin didn't realize the mistake until he got home, so he spent the night reading about magic. He was amazed by what he read

Jean Robert-Houdin was the father of modern magic.

and wanted to learn how to do all the tricks. He later said getting those two books was "the most important event in my life."

Robert-Houdin soon found that he was very good at performing the tricks in the books. When not working on clocks, Robert-Houdin began to perform magic at private parties and small gatherings. Word of his talent quickly spread, and he earned enough money to work on his act full-time. Leaving clock repair behind, he turned his shop into the place where he designed elaborate mechanical magic tricks.

Like Professor Pinetti, Robert-Houdin divided his show into specific acts—one to talk about science, one to demonstrate automata, and another to perform magic. Desiring to learn even more, he became friendly with many magicians performing in shows around Paris. Some of them already knew Robert-Houdin thanks to his automata, and they were happy to teach him their own tricks.

Robert-Houdin was soon a step ahead of most performers of the time because he understood how each act worked: he understood the science displays, he knew the secrets to the magic tricks, and he could build his own automata. To set himself apart from all the others, Robert-Houdin used his knowledge of technology and magic to create one great act.

Robert-Houdin decided that the only place he could do the kind of magic he envisioned was a big theater. In 1845 he opened his own theater in Paris devoted just to magic shows. One of the reasons he wanted his own theater was because of how complicated his show was. The stage itself was an extremely important part of the show. It had to be constructed with special wiring, electricity, lighting, trapdoors, and hidden props. It was outfitted with Robert-Houdin's own automata and allowed him to develop—and keep secret—his own magic tricks.

Similar to Professor Pinetti many decades before him, Robert-Houdin also changed the way magicians looked onstage. If people were going to get dressed up in their finest clothes to come see him perform, then he would dress up just as formally in a suit coat, a top hat, and a tie.

A perfect example of Robert-Houdin's blending of technology and magic was his invention of a trick called the Light and Heavy Chest. He set a small box on a table and invited a member of the audience to pick it up. The person did this easily. Then Robert-Houdin would say a few words over the box and ask the person to

Robert-Houdin's "Light and Heavy Chest"

THE INDIAN ROPE TRICK

Perhaps the most famous trick that no one has ever seen performed is the Indian Rope Trick. It is a simple trick to describe: a magician takes a length of rope and tosses it high into the air. On command, the rope freezes in position, almost like a flagpole. Then an assistant to the magician climbs the rope, which has risen so high that it disappears above the stage curtain, or perhaps into the branches of a tree. When the magician commands the rope to fall back to the ground, the assistant is gone. Apparently, the assistant has climbed so high that he has disappeared into thin air. It's one of the most incredible tricks of all time . . . if it's true.

There were reports of this trick being performed hundreds of years ago in China, and as recently as the 1800s in India. Tellers of this magical tale usually claimed that they saw it performed outside. The only explanation modern magicians have for how the Indian Rope Trick might have been done is if someone up in a tree or on a rooftop was able to grab the rope and hold it steady. Or perhaps it was hooked onto a thin wire already running above the ground.

Nevertheless, to this day, no magician has been able to do this trick and make it believable. Many doubt that it was anything but a magical myth. Thus, the Indian Rope Trick may be one that is forever talked about but never seen.

lift it again. This time it was impossible to lift. In fact, the box wouldn't budge even if a few people tried to move it.

Robert-Houdin accomplished this trick by bringing science in the form of electricity to his act. The box had a metal bottom, and a huge electromagnet was hidden in the table. An electromagnet is a type of extremely strong magnet that is activated when electricity passes through it. While Robert-Houdin was saying his magic words over the box, an assistant hiding offstage flipped a switch that turned on the electromagnet. It was so strong, the metal-bottomed box couldn't be pried away from it—until the switch was turned off. No one who tried to lift the box ever could. But the moment Robert-Houdin stepped back onstage—and signaled his assistant to turn off the magnet—he would pick up the box as if it weighed nothing at all.

Robert-Houdin also was a master mentalist, or mind reader. He was especially good at performing a feat called Second Sight. He would blindfold his assistant—usually his son—Emile, and then ask a spectator to choose a single card from a deck of cards. Robert-Houdin would concentrate on the card and ask his blindfolded assistant to guess what it was. The assistant always guessed correctly.

The act shocked audiences. There was no way the assistant could have seen the card, and Robert-Houdin had not given the assistant any hints as to what the card might be. The audience believed that Robert-Houdin had mysterious mental powers that allowed him to send his thoughts into his assistant's head.

Robert-Houdin's magic was so spectacular and so convincing that the French government hired him as a secret weapon. In 1856

France was in control of Algeria, a country in North Africa. Many Algerians didn't like having the French run their nation, and a small group of Muslim holy men called the Marabouts planned a revolt against the French government. The Marabouts, who believed they had supernatural powers, used tricks like eating glass to prove to other Algerians that they had the power to defeat the French.

The French government sent Robert-Houdin to Africa to show the Algerians that he possessed greater powers than the Marabout magicians. He performed the Light and Heavy Chest Trick on one of the Marabouts. Robert-Houdin allowed the man to lift the box, then supposedly put a spell on him that drained all the energy out of the man. When the Algerian magician tried to lift the box again, he failed. Robert-Houdin then added a little more electricity to the box so that it gave the man a shock. The magician screamed in pain. The Algerians were stunned to see that someone from France had such incredible powers. They decided not to rebel against the French. Robert-Houdin, a magician, became a national hero.

TRICK
3

SECOND SIGHT

Secret Code

SECOND SIGHT, or mind reading, is the ability to guess an object's identity while being blindfolded. It is easy to perform but requires some advance practice with another person. It takes two because you need one person to select the object and the other to guess what it is.

Let's say the magician is the one blindfolded, and the assistant is in the audience. The assistant takes a cell phone from a person in the audience and asks the magician to identify the object. The magician does it quickly. The trick is done again, and the correct answer is given no matter whether the assistant holds up keys, a wallet, a dollar bill, a pair of sunglasses, a book—anything. How is this done when the magician can't see the object?

The secret is all in how the assistant poses the question to the magician. The assistant and magician have a prearranged code that allows them to quickly figure out what the object is. Here's a sample list of codes you can use. Note that each question asks the same thing but is phrased in a unique way. It's up to the magician and the assistant to remember the codes.

"I'm holding an object in my hand. Can you tell me what it is?" (cell phone)

"I have in my hand an object. Can you identify it?" (wallet)

"Can you guess what I am holding in my hand?" (book)

"I'd like you to guess the object I've got in my hand. Can you do that?" (sunglasses)

"Can you tell me the name of the object I'm holding?" (ring)

You get the idea. Additional code words can be used to help identify certain features, like color. Once the object is identified—let's say it's a cell phone—the assistant can describe it with code words for color. For instance the word *nice* would mean "blue," the word *pretty* would mean "black," the word *cool* would mean "silver," and on and on. This takes a lot of memorizing, but it is a marvelous trick two people can perform.

The most amazing practitioner of Second Sight was a man named Charles Morritt. Morritt and his sister, Lilian, were able to perform Second Sight without asking questions. Morritt would simply ask a person from the audience for an object, thank the person who handed it to him, and occasionally mutter words like *please* or *thank you* out loud. There were no other words that could have acted as codes, but Lilian—sitting blindfolded on the stage—was always able to identify the object.

It was a tremendous feat, and Morritt never revealed how he performed it. Modern magicians believe Morritt and his sister had created a code based on time, and every second that passed between the words Morritt muttered signaled a different object. It's amazing to think the two of them could keep perfect time in their minds, without looking at a clock or watch, in order to pull off the trick.

CHAPTER FOUR

STEALING SECRETS AND SUMMONING SPIRITS

URING HIS TEN YEARS AS A PERFORMER, ROBERT-HOUDIN became world famous for his magic, but his popularity made other magicians jealous. They wanted to learn his tricks. They were willing to pay him for the secret to the tricks. But Robert-Houdin wasn't about to sell his secrets, because then everyone could do what he did. That would ruin his career. Unfortunately, Robert-Houdin's refusal to sell didn't stop others from doing everything they could to get access to his secrets . . . even if it involved breaking the law.

One of Robert-Houdin's rivals was a man named John Henry Anderson. He was a magician from Scotland who called himself the Great Wizard of the North. While Robert-Houdin was becoming popular on the European continent, Anderson was building his own theaters in England and Scotland and traveling with his act to North America and Australia.

Anderson was a smart businessman and the first magician to really understand the value of advertising. He created posters and placed ads in newspapers to announce he would be performing in local towns. These advertisements promised readers they would

The Bullet Catch

see amazing things they had never seen before. Anderson was always true to his word—and his advertisements.

His magic was something most people had never seen before and would probably never see again. For example, one trick he performed has come to be known as the Bullet Catch, which is one of the most dangerous magic tricks ever performed. It is still done today, and it is still extremely dangerous.

In this trick, Anderson asked a member of the audience to fire a pistol at his head, claiming that he would catch the speeding bullet with his teeth. This trick made audiences excited, nervous, and scared all at the same time. There were reports that some people fainted from fear at the possibility of seeing someone die onstage. Yet each time the trigger was pulled, the bullet ended up safely in Anderson's teeth. Audiences gasped in relief before applauding wildly.

The Great Wizard of the North was also the first magician to advertise a trick that has since come to define magic: pulling a rabbit out of a hat. No one is certain whether Anderson invented the trick, but he made it one of the most popular conjuring tricks of all time.

Anderson had begun performing before Robert-Houdin had

and was initially more famous. But after traveling the world for several years, he returned to England to find that people were talking about how great Robert-Houdin was. Anderson must have been quite disappointed, but not for long. In a surprising turn of events, Anderson started performing tricks Robert-Houdin had created for his own act—tricks supposedly only Robert-Houdin knew the secrets to.

Something nasty had become part of the magic business: magicians against magicians. In the years ahead, magicians would frequently accuse one another of stealing tricks. Honest magicians started going to court to protect their secrets, while dishonest magicians would do almost anything to steal a trick. They would bribe assistants to tell them how a trick was done or hire spies to sneak into a theater and examine equipment. To them, all that mattered was having the latest and greatest magic as part of their show.

Robert-Houdin found that one of his assistants, a man who helped him build

John Henry Anderson,
"The Great Wizard of the North"

A Robert-Houdin poster

his devices, had secretly made copies of his plans and sold them to other magicians. It is possible that Anderson got these plans and used them to create an act that competed directly with Robert-Houdin's.

While double-crossing assistants were usually at the root of one magician gaining access to another's tricks, some performers delighted in openly exposing others' secrets. One incredibly successful magician of the 1800s got his start in magic by showing how other magicians did their tricks. His name was John Nevil Maskelyne. He was born in England in 1839 and, similar to Robert-Houdin, had worked as a watchmaker as a young man.

TOOLS OF THE TRADE: ASSISTANTS

Magicians in stage shows rely on their assistants to help them perform tricks. Assistants help make the performance a success by creating distractions or by carrying some of the tools the magician needs. Harry Houdini, the great escape artist, employed his wife as his assistant, even though the audience didn't know it. She would pass him small tools just before he was locked up for a particular performance, making it seem as if she were just wishing him good luck with a kiss or an embrace. Modern stage magicians like David Copperfield have assistants who actually look like them, so when they are both dressed in the same clothes (and sometimes a hat), the assistant can appear quickly somewhere else to make it look like the magician is in two places at once.

When you see a magician ask for a volunteer from the audience, most of the time that volunteer is an assistant who works for the magician rather than a random choice. These people know how the trick works and know the right things to say and do to make it look like they're just as amazed by the magic as the audience. In reality, they're putting on a very good act . . . because they are part of the act.

While the audience is focused on the magician, the assistant (or several assistants) can do things onstage that aren't noticed. They can block the audience's view of a mirror, for instance, or walk in front of the magician while he hides something in a pocket. Interestingly, assistants rarely speak. That would make it look like they were trying to distract you. But when they hurry across the stage or present props to the magician with grand sweeping gestures, we don't think of them as much more than busy workers on the stage. That helps disguise their real purpose, which is to make you think they're not really a part of the trick.

But they almost always are.

Maskelyne didn't start his magic career intending to reveal the stage antics of performing magicians. Initially, he delighted in exposing the tricks of people called spiritualists. These men and women—and even some children—claimed to have the power to communicate with ghosts and the spirit world. They would sit in rooms or auditoriums and allow themselves to be blindfolded, tied to chairs, or locked in large cabinets. Then the room would be darkened and the spiritualists would pretend they were

John Nevil Maskelyne gained fame for his ability to levitate people.

talking to dead people. Mysterious sounds, like banging on the walls or blaring trumpets, would fill the darkened room and frighten the audience. Since the spiritualists were tied or locked up, no one could figure out who—or what—was making all the strange noise. The spectators believed that these spiritualists had contact with the dead.

The most famous spiritualist stunt was known as the Magic Cabinet. It was made famous in the mid-1800s by the Davenport Brothers, two early American spiritualists. In front of an audience, Ira and William Henry Davenport were tied up inside a seemingly normal cabinet, and the doors were closed. The lights in the room were dimmed. Suddenly strange illuminated hands were seen reaching out from a hole in the cabinet, accompanied by bizarre knocking sounds and music. When the noises stopped, the lights were turned on. When the cabinet was opened, the Davenports were still tied up. The brothers claimed that while they were tied up in knots, spirits had made all the noise.

The magic cabinets were very simple devices. Almost all magic cabinets—even those used today—were based on two things: a false back that swung open like a door, and a set of mirrors. With the false back, people could climb in and out of the box without the audience seeing them, as long as the front doors were closed.

The mirrors were a little trickier to manage. Magicians and spiritualists used precise geometric calculations to position mirrors at an angle inside the cabinet in such a way that anyone

Spiritualists Ira and Henry Davenport

Mᴿ IRA DAVENPORT.   Mᴿ FAY.   Mᴿ COOPER.   Mᴿ Wᴹ DAVENPORT.

The Davenport brothers and their spirit cabinet
(with assistant William Fay and author Robert Cooper)

looking at an open cabinet would see a reflection of the inside walls of the cabinet. The members of the audience could not see themselves or anything else reflected, so the cabinet looked like an empty cabinet right up to moment the Davenports stepped inside of it. The mirrors helped conceal the false doors and props needed to make the trick work.

It was a good trick, although the Davenports would not admit it was a trick. And from the 1850s to the 1870s, people fell for it.

Maskelyne delighted in showing his audiences there was nothing supernatural about what spiritualists did. They were just very clever magicians who could untie themselves quickly in the dark,

TRICKS OF THE TRADE: MIRRORS

Mirrors are very important because of the way they make our eyes believe we're seeing something that isn't really there. The first mirrors used in magic were actually large pieces of glass used to show human spirits floating onstage.

It was a simple illusion, and one you can demonstrate in your own house. Try this: on a dark night, look out the window of your bedroom or living room with all the lights on *inside*. What do you see? You don't see trees or telephone poles or parked cars *outside*; you see your own reflection. This is because the light from inside your house is reflecting off the glass, and the reflected image is brighter than the objects out in the dark night.

This same principle was used for early magic shows to create the illusion of ghosts and spirits. The audience would sit in front of the stage, looking up at the magician. A very clean sheet of glass was placed across part of the stage, which the audience couldn't see. As lights were lowered on the stage, the tilted glass would reflect the images of the magician's helpers who were in the orchestra pit. The audience couldn't see these people down below because of the raised front wall of the stage.

Up on the stage, it would look like these people were floating in the air as their images reflected upward to the tilted glass. As the magician walked behind the glass, it looked like he was walking right through the spirits.

make lots of noise while moving around the stage (including taking a quick blow on a horn), and retie themselves before the lights came back on.

Maskelyne gained fame by duplicating the spiritualists' tricks in public, showing how they could untie themselves or be let out of the cabinets. This exposure infuriated the spiritualists, and their audiences disappeared after their fraud was exposed. Having successfully revealed the secrets of the spiritualists, Maskelyne began to create tricks of his own. He took over a small theater in London called the Egyptian Hall. There he constructed a show based on his own version of the Magic Cabinet. For his trick, a person entered the cabinet (actually a small closet) and then disappeared. Or someone else appeared in the closet in his or her place. And he did it on a lighted stage, not in a darkened room.

To make the act more interesting, he created fanciful stories and dramatic plays with exotic themes that led up to someone disappearing in the cabinet. Maskelyne's illusion was helped by the fact that the theaters were dark and smoky.

Nonetheless, by the end of the nineteenth century other smart magicians had figured out how to build their own magic cabinets. This upset Maskelyne to no end, and he went to court several times to protect his version of the cabinet. By then it was too late for his act. Most of his competitors knew the secret . . . and they had started using it. Hurt by all the copycats, Maskelyne was determined to create something no one else could copy. The success of his theater depended on it. He settled on the idea of making objects levitate. Maskelyne had seen other magicians make objects such as brooms and silverware float in the air. He knew that thin black wires were used to make these objects drift across the stage. These tricks were audience favorites because no one could see the black wires.

Levitation was interesting, but the objects themselves were boring. What if he could make a person float through the air? Maskelyne wondered. He believed it would be the most remarkable trick in history. But an average person weighed more than a hundred pounds. That would be much more difficult than making a bottle or broom or a bouquet of roses float around. Lifting something as heavy as a young man or woman would require lots of machinery.

Maskelyne set about creating the illusion. After many months of preparation, in 1897, he unveiled a play called *Trapped by Magic*, which ended with the levitation of a man who rose off the stage. To make sure no one thought the man was suspended by wires or propped up on a stand, Maskelyne ran a huge hoop over the length of the man's body, proving that he was floating by himself. In later shows, Maskelyne improved his levitation trick by having the floating person move around the stage.

The levitation trick invented by Maskelyne is one of the most awe-inspiring tricks in all magic. You and I know that people can't float in the air. It's impossible. Gravity does not allow heavy objects, like a human body, to rise off the ground. The only way something heavy can be lifted into the air is if something is lifting it or is pushing it upward. And just because a magician's machinery can't be seen by the audience, doesn't mean it's not there.

Making someone levitate is a good example of a trick that must be done on a stage. You won't see a street performer levitating a

KELLAR

LEVITATION.

A poster for Harry Kellar shows the magician performing levitation.

spectator, because it requires special equipment that would be seen outside in the sunlight. This equipment includes simple devices such as pulleys and thin wires covered with paint so they won't shine and very sophisticated machines that can push a body upward using metal poles. The machinery that made Maskelyne's trick possible was so complicated—it had dozens and dozens of wires coming up from the floor and down from the ceiling—that it took a long time before any other magicians figured out how he did it.

Maskelyne had the most successful show in all of England for many years. He eventually employed other magicians to be part of a traveling show that performed in other countries while Maskelyne was in England.

TRICK ★4★

LEVITATION

NO MATTER who's doing it, levitation requires machinery or a very sturdy prop. In Maskelyne's day, wires were used to suspend the person being levitated. Today, everything from wires to mechanical lifts are used. Yet with the right tools and supervision, this trick can be done by almost anyone. Here's a look at a simple levitation table that works perfectly well but doesn't have any moving parts.

Note that the placement of the curtain (which covers the strut supporting the table) is crucial to making the trick look realistic. The same is true for the sawhorse supports. They don't do anything except provide the illusion that they're holding the table up. In fact, they're barely touching the table. Also, the magician has to walk around the table as if nothing is blocking his way. This makes it appear as if nothing is supporting the table other than the sawhorses.

Once the assistant is on the table, the magician leans over, appearing to hypnotize or convey some powers to the assistant. This leaning adds to the effect that there is nothing in the magician's path. After this magical transference, the magician removes the sawhorses, one at a time, and the table is left floating. The magician waves his hands over and under the table, being careful not to bump the support. Once it's proved that the table is floating, the magician replaces the sawhorses and helps the assistant off the table, and the trick is completed.

CHAPTER FIVE

THE ONE HOUDINI AND ONLY

BEFORE HE DIED, JEAN ROBERT-HOUDIN, THE FRENCH father of modern magic, wrote several books, including one titled *Memoirs of Robert-Houdin, Ambassador, Author, and Conjurer. Written by Himself.* In this book, published in 1859, Robert-Houdin explained how he had created many of his magic tricks, finally giving away the secrets others had tried to buy or steal from him. The book revealed how he built his automata and how he created the Second Sight act. Robert-Houdin's autobiography became a textbook for future generations of magicians, much as *The Discoverie of Witchcraft* had been three centuries before.

Robert-Houdin's book influenced many magicians, but it literally changed one boy's life forever. The boy was Ehrich Weiss. He was born in Budapest, Austria-Hungary, on March 24, 1874, at the height of the great European magic shows. Yet Ehrich never saw any of them because his family moved to America when he was only four. The Weiss family first settled in Appleton, Wisconsin, before moving to New York City.

As a kid, Ehrich did a number of odd jobs to help his family make money. The ones he enjoyed most involved performing in front of crowds, especially as a side-walk acrobat and a trapeze artist. He spent his free time reading and rereading Robert-Houdin's autobi-ography, learning all he could. He was so impressed with what Robert-Houdin had done as a magician that at age seventeen, he changed his own name to resemble Robert-Houdin's. Adding an *i* to Robert-Houdin's name, Ehrich began calling himself Harry Houdini. The name made him sound as if he were related to the magician he idolized.

A portrait of Harry Houdini, c. 1913.

While living in New York City, Houdini initially worked at a "normal" job in a necktie factory. When he felt he was a good enough magician, he quit to perform card tricks in a vaudeville-style show at the Coney Island amusement park. He also got occasional magic jobs at the circuses, theaters, and sideshows that were scattered throughout New York. These were small shows that promised visitors unusual and even bizarre sights.

Some were genuinely strange, like two-headed cows, and some were kind of sad, like conjoined twins and bearded ladies.

Vaudeville shows created new opportunities for magicians.

Vaudeville shows had changed the way magic acts had to be performed. During the 1800s, many magicians had surrounded their tricks with stories and plays to make the magic more entertaining. But audiences grew tired of listening to the long stories while waiting for the actual trick. Th eir attention was captured instead by vaudeville shows, which started appearing all over the United States in the 1880s. These were theater performances that presented different types of entertainment very quickly one after another. A single night of vaudeville might feature a singing group, a juggler, a comedian, a magician, an animal show, and a family of acrobats. And the action never stopped, as each act hurried onstage the moment the previous one was over.

Vaudeville completely changed the way audiences thought

about a night of entertainment. Why should they pay to see one magician in his own show when they could go to a vaudeville show and see a dozen different acts for the same price?

Magicians in need of work joined vaudeville shows and focused their acts on individual tricks. In a sense, magic was going backward. It had gone from the streets and small table-tops to huge theaters and stage spectacles, and now was back to competing for attention with jugglers and musicians.

In this environment, Houdini's tricks were nothing extraordinary. He tried to impress people with simple card tricks and called himself the "King of Cards." There was, however, one thing Houdini was extremely good at: picking locks and getting out of handcuffs. He had learned the basics of escaping from other magicians he worked with, but he spent long hours alone examining the inner design of locks so he understood exactly how they worked. He developed a keen understanding of lock construction and learned how to open them with everyday objects. For example, he figured out that many handcuffs could be unlocked using the tips of shoestrings. They could also be opened by banging them forcefully against a hard object like a desk or a wall.

In 1893, when Harry was nineteen, he and his brother Theo, also a small-time magician, performed as a duo called the Brothers Houdini. Many of their performances featured Harry escaping from locked trunks and police handcuffs. Theo would lock Harry's hands in the cuffs, put him in a big cloth sack, and lock him in a large trunk. Theo would then stand on top of the trunk and hold a drape in front of him. After saying a few words to the audience, he would lift the drape over his head, concealing him and the trunk. In a matter of seconds, when the drape was lowered, the person holding it was Harry. When Harry opened the trunk, it was Theo who was inside the sack with handcuffs on his wrists.

While performing with Theo, Harry met a woman named Wilhelmina Beatrice Rahner, known as Bess. She was a singer and dancer in some of the venues where the Brothers Houdini put on their show. Harry and Bess dated briefly, fell in love, and were married in 1894. From that point forward, they were an inseparable couple.

Harry's ability to break any lock attracted people to see the

Houdini with his mother, Cecilia, and wife, Bess

Houdinis, and the brothers became popular with crowds in New York. But Theo eventually left the act to perform on his own. Harry chose his wife, already a seasoned performer, to become his new magic partner. Harry and Bess performed all around New York for years, but their life was difficult, and the crowds got smaller and smaller as time went on. The couple had to move into Harry's mother's house because he could not get enough work to pay their rent. In 1899, with a new century looming, he thought he had gone as far as he could, even though he was only twenty-five years old. He considered giving up magic altogether. Perhaps, he thought, he could use his skills to become a locksmith.

However, in one of those strokes of luck that change a life, a gentleman named Martin Beck happened to see the part of Houdini's act where Harry escaped from handcuffs. Beck was very impressed. He owned a string of vaudeville theaters and was interested in getting stage acts for his venues. Beck told Houdini that if he focused his act on one thing—escaping—he would book Houdini in vaudeville shows all over the country.

Despite wanting desperately to perform all types of magic, Houdini agreed. As Beck predicted, Houdini soon became popular with crowds who couldn't believe

Theater owner Martin Beck persuaded Houdini to focus his career on escapes.

he could get out of locked boxes, layers of chains, knotted ropes, and steel handcuffs. It seemed as if nothing could hold Houdini. He was so good that he dared anyone in the audience, including policemen, to bring their own locks and handcuffs to bind him. They did, and Houdini easily got out of all of them.

Suddenly Houdini was a one-of-a-kind magician. No one else performed solely as an escapologist. Many magicians did hand-cuff tricks, but they didn't climb into locked trunks or escape from chains. Houdini did all these things, and he was the best.

He was also a smart businessman. Like the Great Wizard of the North, Robert-Houdin, and other magicians before him,

Houdini chained for a movie role

*Muscles and chains were important parts
of Houdini's persona.*

Houdini knew the value of advertising and publicity. While he was performing in San Francisco, he told reporters that even the San Francisco police department couldn't find a way to keep him locked up. The police responded by inviting Houdini to prove it. The challenge made headlines in the newspapers.

Houdini went to the police department, with reporters following, and told the police to chain him up with whatever they had. To make it more interesting, he added a twist. He would first strip naked and allow the police to search him for anything that might act as a key or a pick to break the locks. They did and then wrapped him in chains, locks, and handcuffs.

Houdini was put in a cell, and the crowd was led outside to wait. After only a few minutes Houdini walked out completely free. The locks and chains were lying on the floor. Houdini had escaped from everything the police had tried to shackle him with.

Pictures of Houdini without his shirt appeared the next day in the papers, and he immediately became a celebrity. Houdini wasn't surprised: he had planned everything perfectly. He knew that his naked stunt would attract attention because it would prove he wasn't using special tools to escape (although even a naked man can hide a key in his mouth or between his toes), and he also knew that he looked good in photographs. Houdini was short, but he had the stout shape of a bodybuilder, with a strong chest and arm muscles. The newspapers were happy to print pictures of a handsome escape artist who had outwitted the police—that kind of story was sure to sell lots of newspapers. It all helped make Houdini famous.

Houdini's muscles were not about vanity; they were important to his act. Houdini's ability to puff up his chest and to flex his muscles actually helped him escape from chains. When he was being bound, he would inhale lots of air and tense his muscles, making his chest and arms swell. After the chains or ropes were in place, he would relax and let his lungs deflate. This made his chest and arms smaller, and caused the manacles to slide off more easily.

Oddly enough, the same body structure that helped him make incredible escapes was probably part of the reason Houdini was never a great Sleight of Hand magician. His hands, wrists, and fingers might have been too thick and not quick enough to make him truly great at card tricks.

But card tricks were all in the past. A single year had changed Houdini's life: he'd gone from wanting to give up on magic to touring Europe. He became an international celebrity, an entertainer who was treated with the same respect given to popular writers, actors and actresses, and singers and dancers. Yet the more famous he became, the more daring he had to make his stunts. When he realized that his handcuff escapes were becoming too familiar—and perhaps even boring—to his audiences, Houdini started using straitjackets. These are coats with long sleeves and lots of straps. The long sleeves are tied behind the wearer's back, and the straps keep the wearer from getting out of the jacket. They are used for people who may be very violent or hard to control, such as angry prisoners. Houdini's advertisements claimed that he could escape from these garments used for "the murderous insane." People showed up to see him wrestle desperately against the tight sleeves and heavy straps. It seemed as if he himself was violent or insane as he thrashed about the stage fighting to free himself. Of course, he always got free.

Houdini came up with the idea that if people thought he was in real danger—that he might even die—he would attract even more attention. The audience members had to be afraid for him, and hope that they never experienced the situation themselves. In perhaps the most brilliant move of his career, Houdini decided to use a universal human fear in his act: the fear of suffocating to death.

He created a trick simply known as the Milk Can Escape. Before modern grocery stores sold milk bottles or milk cartons, milk was stored in big metal cans about three feet high. They were just big enough for a person to

Houdini inside the infamous milk can

squish into. As part of Houdini's new act, a milk can would be filled to the top with water. Houdini would be handcuffed, climb into the can, and then crouch down. His assistant would push his head under the water and lock the top of the can. A curtain was pulled in front of the can. After several suspenseful minutes, Houdini would appear. He was gasping for breath as if he'd almost died. Crowds loved it because Houdini appeared to have done the impossible—he had cheated death.

To heighten the suspense, Houdini told his audience members to begin holding their breaths the instant he was locked in the can. Most of them couldn't hold their breath for more than a minute. As they sucked in big gulps of air, they knew that Houdini must be running out of air himself, especially locked in a small container full of water. They thought he was drowning right in front of them.

The fact was that Houdini was never in any danger. For years he had practiced holding his breath and could easily hold it for several minutes. Once in the water, he was able to unlock the handcuffs and remove the top of the can in less than a minute, but he remained underwater as long as he could, knowing that the audience members had already given up holding their own breaths—and that they believed he couldn't possibly hold his own much longer.

Every few months Houdini found some new way to make people think his act put him in grave danger. He had himself chained and handcuffed and thrown into icy rivers, or put into a sack and tossed into lakes. On September 26, 1911, Houdini performed his oddest escape. A dead "sea monster" weighing nearly a ton had been brought ashore in Boston, and several residents dared Houdini to crawl into the dead beast and try to escape from it. In reality, the monster was probably a giant squid, an incredibly rare sea creature that hardly ever comes to the ocean's surface.

The squid was dragged onstage at the theater where Houdini was performing. His legs and arms were chained, and he was forced inside the creature by his assistants. Then the sea monster was sewn shut with metal wire, and chains were wrapped around its body. A curtain was pulled around it, and the audience waited for Houdini to emerge. When he did, fifteen minutes later, he was covered in the beast's slimy fluids.

One strategy Houdini used with the sea monster trick was to reattach all the locks and chains after he had emerged but before the curtain was pulled aside. He did this with most of his tricks. With the locks and chains in place, it gave the impression that he had magically found his way through his shackles without ever actually opening them. To many people, this was a sign that Houdini had supernatural powers.

Emerging from the sea monster may have been his strangest stunt, but in 1912 Houdini introduced his most famous trick, one that is still used by many escape artists today. It is called the Water Torture Cell, and it was a combination of his best escapes all in one trick. A large glass chamber, like an aquarium, was filled with water. Using ropes, Houdini's assistants lowered him headfirst into the water and then locked the top down. Audiences could see Houdini holding his breath with his head at the bottom of the cell. The assistants stepped away and covered the cell with a curtain. They then stood by with axes, ready to break through the glass if something went wrong.

Minutes later, dripping sheets of water, Houdini would jump out in front of the curtain at the precise moment when everyone thought he was doomed.

The Water Torture Cell was Houdini's most impressive trick, and it gained him worldwide fame, but Houdini was just as well known for his publicity stunts. These were designed to get newspapers to write about him and to attract paying customers to his shows. His greatest stunt may have been the Suspended Straitjacket. In 1916 in front of a crowd of thousands in Washington, DC, he was tied up in a straitjacket. A crane then lifted him, feetfirst, a hundred feet into the air. Not only did he have to get out of the straitjacket, but he also had to keep from falling to the concrete below.

After several tense minutes when it looked like Houdini might fail, he finally escaped from the straitjacket. Then he climbed the rope to the top of the crane, where he stood victorious up in the sky. When he threw his straitjacket down to the people below, they screamed their approval.

The secret to Houdini's tricks was very simple: he never let himself be locked up unless he knew beforehand how to get out. He prepared long and hard for every stunt, even those that seemed like on-the-spot challenges, such as the ones from local police departments (these were actually arranged ahead of time). And Bess was extremely important in his plans. Some magicians think Bess would pass Houdini keys with her mouth when she kissed him good-bye—just after he had been searched and just before he began whatever dangerous stunt he was performing.

While Houdini was a master showman and a fantastic escape artist, he was an impatient man in person. He particularly disliked other magicians, most of whom he considered inferior performers. Houdini even wrote a book that claimed his inspiration, Jean Robert-Houdin, was not a particularly good magician. Yet Houdini

The Vanishing Elephant

longed to have the kind of magical skill these men displayed with their illusions. He still wanted to amaze audiences with "real" magic, not just escapes.

The opportunity to pull off a sensational magic trick arrived when Houdini was hired to perform at the Hippodrome in New

York City. The Hippodrome was a huge arena similar to today's indoor stadiums. Houdini performed a trick there that he had never done before. It was called the Vanishing Elephant.

An elephant was brought into the arena and led into a large circus wagon next to where Houdini stood. Once it was completely inside, the doors of the wagon were closed on the beast.

Houdini said a few words and then dramatically pulled the doors of the wagon open. The people sitting near Houdini looked into the wagon and saw nothing except the curtains on the other side of the stage. The wagon was empty; they were looking right through it. There was no elephant.

To this day no one knows exactly how Houdini did the trick. The elephant was too big to drop through a trapdoor, and the audience would have seen the elephant if the animal had tried to sneak out the other side of the wagon. No one knows what happened to the elephant.

To say it was a phenomenal trick would be an understatement. In the years since he performed it, the Vanishing Elephant has been one of magic's biggest mysteries. It is all the more interesting because Houdini was not a very good stage magician. Despite that, he managed to create one of the only illusions modern magicians still haven't completely figured out.

There have been some good guesses, but they are all guesses. The most popular theory is that Houdini used very large mirrors and got some help from Charles Morritt, the famed mentalist. However it came about, Houdini won praise for the magic trick, and his performances at the Hippodrome helped cement his reputation as a complete magician.

As Houdini got older, he appeared in movies and spent a lot of his time exposing spiritualists and those who claimed to talk to the dead in séances (meetings where people chatted with ghosts). But he still performed escapes right up until he died. And his death came not as a result of some dangerous stunt, but as the result of a casual conversation.

In the fall of 1926, Houdini was relaxing on a couch after a show in Montreal, Canada, talking with some college students about how strong his stomach and chest muscles were. One of the students, named J. Gordon Whitehead, asked Houdini if he could stand a direct punch to the stomach. Houdini said he could, and the student hit him several times without warning. Houdini had no time to prepare for the punches, which came hard and fast.

Many doctors today believe that Houdini was already suffering from appendicitis by the time this event happened and that the punches added damage to his body. Houdini didn't realize how ill he was at the time, even though he was in great pain. He traveled to Detroit to perform a show several days later and passed out after the performance.

Houdini was taken to a nearby hospital. By the time surgeons operated on him, it was too late. He had a ruptured appendix and peritonitis, which meant his abdomen was severely infected. Harry died as the infection ravaged his body. He was only fifty-two years old. The date was October 31, 1926. It was, coincidentally, Halloween—the day on which people trick-or-treat. Houdini had been the master of treating people to tricks.

HOUDINI'S CONTEMPORARIES

Houdini's fame was greater than any other magician of his time. There were other incredible magicians of the early 1900s, but none were quite the celebrity that Houdini was. Some of their accomplishments were overshadowed by all the publicity Houdini received. Nonetheless, they created tricks that were every bit as astonishing as Houdini's escapes.

In England, Charles Morritt (of Second Sight fame) returned to the stage after a long absence. He had disappeared from performing for so long that many of his rivals thought he had died. When he took the stage in 1912, it was with an illusion that confused all those rivals—likely the precursor to Houdini's Vanishing Elephant Trick. Morritt's illusion was called, quite descriptively, the Disappearing Donkey. In this trick, a clown led a stubborn donkey into a large wheeled crate, similar to a wagon. Once the donkey was securely inside the crate, the clown jumped out and closed the door.

Morritt walked over and threw open the walls of the crate. The donkey was gone. Now, a donkey is not a small thing. It is a large, stubborn animal. It doesn't take commands like a human assistant. Donkeys have to be led around and told what to do. But it had been alone in the crate. No one could figure out what happened to the donkey. It could not have gone through a trapdoor because the crate was on wheels, which raised the floor of the crate above the stage. It couldn't go out the back because the audience would have seen the donkey standing up and being led away. It was one of the world's most perfect tricks, and it took almost a hundred years until any other magician could figure out how Morritt did it. Of course, if he really did help Houdini, that's a different story.

Even though the storytelling style of John Nevil Maskelyne, the man who invented the human levitation trick, had largely gone out of style by Houdini's time, one of his employees took over Maskelyne's act and became world famous. His name was David Devant, and he was a magician who had helped Maskelyne when the levitation trick was being developed. Devant was a charming man who hit upon the idea of inviting the audience to be part of his act. He would call people out of the audience to assist him with his tricks or to have tricks played on them. His act was popular with audiences of all ages, and in the years before World War I, it made him the only magician who might have been a true rival to Houdini in terms of popularity.

David Devant's act was popular with audiences of all ages.

One of Devant's best tricks was inviting a boy and a girl onto the stage to watch him while he pulled eggs out of an empty hat. He asked

Howard Thurston was invited to perform magic
at the White House.

them to hold the eggs, but he kept reaching into his hat and pulling out more and more. Eventually he loaded up the kids' arms with so many eggs, they couldn't hold them anymore. The eggs usually ended up shattered all across the stage, with the audience laughing hysterically. The Queen of England asked Devant to come and perform this trick especially for her.

The queen wasn't the only head of a country who liked magic. President Calvin Coolidge invited Howard Thurston, one of the most popular magicians in America, to perform at a Christmas dinner party at the White House in 1924. After making various birds and rabbits appear and disappear, Thurston asked to borrow the president's watch. Coolidge looked on with horror as Thurston proceeded to smash the watch, a gift from some politicians in Massachusetts, with a hammer. Facing a stunned room—*how could Thurston have done that to the president's own watch?* they wondered—the magician asked for a loaf of bread to be brought from the kitchen. When Mrs. Coolidge cut it open, the watch was inside, good as new.

A poster for Thurston's version of the levitation trick

TRICK
✳ 5 ✳

THE DISAPPEARING KNOT

ROPES AND KNOTS are not always what they appear to be. There are literally hundreds of knots (shoelace knots, sailor's knots, etc.), and many of them are designed specifically for magic. They might appear to be tight or very strong, but with a little bit of twisting and turning, these types of knots turn out to be illusions—they're not even knots at all. Here's a rope trick featuring what looks like a perfect knot. The knot is, in fact, nothing more than carefully tied loops . . . but the audience won't know that.

Take a length of rope about three or four feet long. To make it easy, think of the end that starts in your left hand as Point A and the one that starts in your right hand as Point Z. Start by bringing Point Z up and over the back of your left hand and over the top of your index finger. Have Point Z pass over Point A and in between your index and middle finger, where it is grasped. Now your index and middle finger are holding Point Z, and Point A is being held in place where Point Z crossed it.

Take your right hand and go through the loop that's hanging below your left hand. Reach up and grab Point A and begin pulling. Grab Point Z with the other fingers of your left hand and begin pulling that in the opposite direction. As the loop slips off your right hand, it will form a knot (but not a real one).

This fake knot is delicate, and to keep it from coming apart under its own weight, you need to gradually roll the rope toward you with the thumb and fingers of each hand (almost as if you were rolling a pen or straw between your fingers).

On command, say a magic word, and pull the rope tight. The knot will have disappeared, and the audience will see a perfectly straight line of rope.

CHAPTER SIX

A CENTURY OF SHOCKS, SCARES, AND SCIENCE

T HE TWENTIETH CENTURY BROUGHT UNIMAGINABLE MARVELS in magic and science to people all over the world. Electric appliances, automobiles, movies, and the very first airplane would all be part of the new millennium.

One individual who created some of these marvels was Nikola Tesla. He was the last man to combine magic and science, much as the alchemists had done hundreds of years before him, and the last scientist to create shows that rivaled those of magicians. His presentations and experiments were even more spectacular than the illusions of Robert-Houdin and Maskelyne, and on a single night in 1899, he may have performed one of the most mysterious tricks of all time.

Tesla was born in what is modern-day Croatia in 1856, but moved to the United States when he was twenty-seven years old. He worked for Thomas Edison and improved on many of Edison's ideas for motors and electrical generators. By the time he was forty years old, Tesla understood electricity better than anyone on the planet.

After Edison refused to pay Tesla some money he owed him,

Nikola Tesla, one of history's greatest scientists

Tesla set out on his own. He was intent on uncovering the mysterious nature of electricity and showing it to the world. At numerous exhibitions, he showed people incredible displays of electricity. During lectures and public presentations, he would hold a fluorescent tube or a lightbulb in his hand and then raise it into the air. It was not connected to any power source. Mysteriously, it would flash to life, blazing brightly as he held it up. This was not magic, Tesla said, but science—he had constructed a machine that could send electricity through the air, and the airborne electricity was creating the light.

These demonstrations were very similar to those given by

magicians like Professor Pinetti. People, including other scientists, actually thought Tesla's displays were magic tricks because they didn't understand the advanced level of science Tesla was working with. To observers, it was no different from magic. Tesla never claimed to be a magician, though. Everything he did—no matter how amazing—was part of his scientific research. In the grand scheme of things, these public displays were a tiny sample of a huge experiment Tesla was working on. He believed that electricity could be transmitted over hundreds or thousands of miles without wires, through the air or even through the earth. He experimented with ways to make this possible.

To test his idea that electricity could be sent to any spot on Earth, Tesla built a huge laboratory in Colorado Springs, Colorado. After much preparation, he was ready to see if he was right. On one night in 1899 his lab lit up with the glare of electricity. Suddenly lightning bolts shot hundreds of feet into the air—lightning bolts created by his machines and power generators. And just as suddenly, all the power in Colorado Springs disappeared. The city went dark. Tesla's huge experiment had zapped the electrical generation system for the entire city. It was damaged so badly that no one, except for Tesla, could fix it.

To this day, no one is quite sure what Tesla achieved that night. He might have actually sent electricity through the air in a way no one had ever done, before or since. Tesla wouldn't discuss the outage because of the damage his experiment caused to the city's power supply. Instead he closed his lab, locked his research papers away, and moved to New York City to continue his experiments.

In New York he amazed his friends, including Mark Twain, with demonstrations of how he could control bursts of electricity and cause things to glow. He built a small boat that could be controlled from the shore (the first remote-controlled toy), and he started a small earthquake with a device he carried in his pocket. Most people couldn't begin to understand how Tesla did these things.

None of it was magic, but Tesla showed how science could be even more mysterious than magic. Today the things he invented are part of our everyday lives, like radio and the remote control, but a hundred years ago they seemed like magic of the most spectacular sort. Tesla came up with the idea of how to harness electricity so it could be sent from generating stations over wires to homes and buildings. Unfortunately, inventors like Thomas Edison and radio pioneer Guglielmo Marconi were better businessmen than Tesla and took credit for some of the things he invented.

When Tesla died, he was working on something he thought of as a peace ray, but that the media called a death ray. According to Tesla, it was a concentrated beam of energy that could stop anything right in its tracks, even if it were hundreds of feet away. Tesla believed if every country had one of these peace rays, then wars would no longer be possible.

However, the device was never completed. It has been a source of interest to people ever since Tesla described it, because moments after he died in 1943, the U.S. government and the FBI collected all his papers and locked them away so no one would ever see them, claiming they were top secret.

Like the tricks of an astonishing magician, Tesla's greatest secrets may never be revealed. There is no doubt he was one of the most important scientists and inventors of all time. He did find ways to control nature—in the form of electricity—just as the ancient magicians were alleged to have done. Even though he was a scientist, his flair for showmanship made his work as exciting as that ever done by stage magicians. Perhaps Tesla understood the relationship between science and magic better than anyone who ever lived.

In the years immediately after World War I, magicians struggled to find new ways to bring people into their shows. It was hard to compete with movies or riding around town in a new car. Maskelyne's levitation trick had been the last really impressive illusion, and even that had been figured out by other magicians. American magician Harry Kellar had reportedly walked onstage while Maskelyne was performing the levitation to see for himself how it was done. By the 1920s, every magic show worth seeing now had its own levitation trick.

London magician P. T. Selbit knew he would have to go beyond levitation to get people to come to his show.

P. T. Selbit scared audiences with his magic.

TOOLS OF THE TRADE: ELECTRICITY

Electricity has been a part of stage magic since the mid-1800s, usually for a specific trick or to operate hidden machinery. But a Scottish magician named Walford Bodie made electricity the centerpiece of his magic show. In the early 1900s, using static electricity (which is relatively harmless), Bodie would cause sparks to shoot from people who were sitting onstage. He hooked wires up to members of the audience and then had them hold lightbulbs, which would light up in their hands. Bodie even used an actual electric chair from a prison. He had people sit in it while he performed tricks, making the audience feel like there was the possibility that something "shocking" was going to happen. No one was ever in danger, because electricity only flowed when Bodie pressed his foot on certain sections of the stage, although the audience wasn't aware of this little detail.

Bodie went too far, though, when he began claiming that his electrical abilities could cure people of disease. His shows turned into fake "faith healing" events during which he would pretend to cure handicapped people of their disabilities with electricity and hypnosis. He called this "bloodless surgery." He even added the letters *MD* to his name. To most of the world, this means "medical doctor," but when confronted about being a doctor, Bodie said that *MD* simply stood for Merry Devil. This bit of dishonesty got Bodie into trouble with the law, and he was taken to court. Like many great magicians, however, he emerged unscathed and continued to perform.

As people became more familiar with electricity—from lightbulbs to appliances—Bodie's act eventually became less impressive, and he played smaller and smaller halls until his death in 1939.

The "electrifying" Walford Bodie

decided it would take something scary, perhaps a little gory, and altogether terrifying. Selbit had just the thing.

Selbit was born Percy Thomas Tibbles in 1881. He chose the stage name of P. T. Selbit by spelling his last name backward and dropping a *b*. And he had received a most interesting introduction to magic: as a boy he worked for a silversmith in the same building where Charles Morritt—who created the Disappearing Donkey and possibly the Vanishing Elephant—built his stage tricks. Whenever Morritt was away, the young P. T. would sneak into Morritt's workshop and figure out how the tricks worked.

He began performing magic shows in 1902, working for a time with Maskelyne and Devant. But, like many magicians, he saw that people were gradually losing interest in magic shows. Selbit realized that he had to do something outrageous to attract audiences. He began inventing tricks based on what he thought people wanted to see. One thing he realized was that frightening people went a long way toward getting more of them to come to his act. The popularity of horror movies, roller-coaster rides, and haunted houses proved that. Selbit also understood that people are curious about things that are unpleasant, like traffic accidents and even death. Selbit incorporated both of these human elements—fear and curiosity—into a trick he performed in 1921 that ended up being every bit as amazing as Maskelyne's levitation.

Selbit called his trick Sawing Through a Woman. It was exactly what it sounded like; Selbit didn't give it a fantastic name or a mystical story. The name of the trick was what people were going to see—a woman cut in half by a saw.

Selbit placed a woman in a box that looked like a coffin and tied her arms and feet with rope so she could not move. The rope was pulled out through holes in the box and held by his assistants to make sure the woman didn't try to push her way out of the box. He dropped the lid, covering the woman. Selbit would then sternly instruct two assistants to saw through the middle of the box.

The men grunted as they struggled to cut all the way through. Bits of wood and sawdust splintered into the air. When they finally cut through the bottom and pulled the saw away, the audience believed that the woman had been cut right through her waist.

As the audience gasped in horror, Selbit walked back to the box, acting very serious. He opened it as if expecting to find it filled with blood and body parts. Instead he reached his hand in and helped the woman out. She was smiling . . . and still in one piece.

It was a brilliant spectacle for many reasons. First of all, it featured a woman. Women were not usually included in illusions onstage because the big bulky dresses fashionable at the time made it difficult for women to move quickly around a stage crowded with props.

Women were also getting the political and social rights they had long fought for, like the right to vote. Women's rights were still controversial, though, and many people were uncomfortable with women commanding more attention than they ever had. Selbit played on this concern by making a woman the centerpiece of his act.

Second, Selbit made the people in the audience feel like they were sneaking a look at something inappropriate. It was almost as if they were watching something that was against the law. To add to this sense of the inappropriate, between his shows Selbit had his

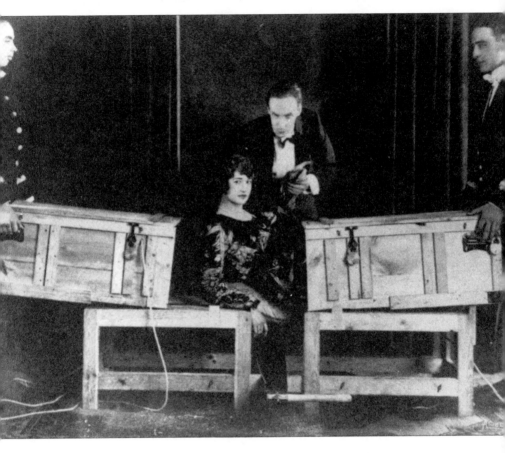

Selbit performing Sawing Through a Woman

assistants pour buckets of what looked like blood in the gutters outside the theater—as if they were cleaning up after something horrible. He also parked an ambulance outside to make it appear that his show could potentially result in a tragic medical emergency.

Separating a human into parts was as great a trick as making people levitate. People couldn't figure out how it was done, and Selbit's addition of theatrical horror made it all the more popular. As we've seen, though, popularity leads to thievery and copycats. Sawing Through a Woman was soon being performed by other magicians. Selbit ended up spending much of his time in court trying to protect the trick he had created.

Ambulances waited outside Selbit's performances.

WHERE ARE ALL THE FEMALE MAGICIANS?

It is probably apparent as you read through these pages that there is little mention of women in magic—other than as assistants or partners. In many ways, magic—like other performance arts—has reflected the way society felt about the roles of men and women (consider Selbit sawing a woman in half during the women's suffrage movement).

As magic became a legitimate form of entertainment—and not just an offshoot of witchcraft and petty crimes—magicians began sharing their secrets with apprentices and occasionally their peers. This led to the formation of small private clubs and organizations dedicated to promoting magic and preserving the knowledge of how to perform tricks. Like many exclusive organizations of the nineteenth and early twentieth centuries—political parties, unions, university clubs, business service groups—these gatherings of magicians were open only to men. The male members of magic societies passed on their tricks to male confidants or male apprentices usually by word of mouth and always very cautiously. Women were prohibited from joining any groups where secrets were shared. While this policy has changed in the past few decades, many of the magic societies are still dominated by men.

Of course, like anything that evolves, magic is changing. The world of magic is finally embracing female magicians, whether as solo acts or as equal partners of male magicians. In the United States alone there are now hundreds of women performing as professional magicians. They are every bit as skilled as their male peers, and they have adapted traditional magic to make it their own. It is only a matter of time until a female magician becomes just as famous in her time as Houdini was in his.

CUTTING A PERSON IN HALF

THERE ARE NUMEROUS ways to cut a person in half. Of course, none involves really cutting into the person. One way is to have two people curled up in opposite ends of the box. Another involves having the assistant's body sink down into the table the box is resting on so the assistant's body is actually underneath the box when it's cut.

The most famous method for Cutting a Person in Half may be one that involves a single person and two fake feet. Remember the automata figures and how lifelike they were even hundreds of years ago? Well, feet can be automata, too. Fake toes can be made to wriggle like real ones with a tiny

set of springs and gears. As the magician twirls the box to show all sides to the audience, the person in the box slides fake feet into the slots when the end of the box is facing away from the audience.

There's a paper version of the Cutting a Person in Half Trick that is similarly cool, and you can do it almost anywhere.

Take a strip of paper and an envelope.

Seal the envelope closed.

Draw a picture of a person on the entire length of the paper.

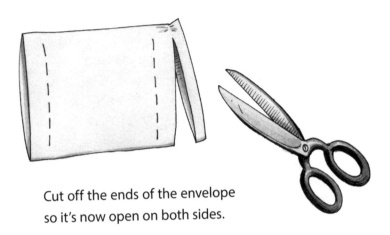

Cut off the ends of the envelope
so it's now open on both sides.

Slide your picture into the
envelope....

 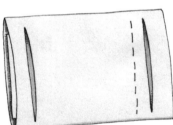

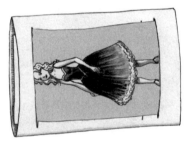

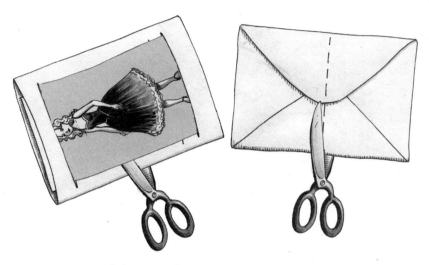

and then cut the envelope up the middle.

As soon as you've done this, dramatically pull out the picture of the person to show it is completely unharmed. And once you've done this, show that the entire envelope is cut in two, to prove you didn't just cut the top part of the envelope.

Like all great tricks, the magic is in the preparation. Before you do the trick, cut two slits into the front of the envelope, but don't let anyone see them. When you slip the picture of the person into the envelope, make sure it comes out of the first slit and back into the second one. That means the middle of it is outside the envelope while you're cutting the envelope. When you show your audience that you've truly cut it in half, crumple up the two pieces and throw them away so that no one can examine them.

CHAPTER SEVEN

AN OASIS APPEARS
IN THE DESERT

OR FOUR DECADES, FROM THE 1930S TO THE 1960S, THERE was little interest in magic. With no places like the grand Egyptian Hall in London or Robert-Houdin's theater in Paris dedicated to magic, it seemed as if magic as a spectacle had all but vanished from the face of the earth.

The popularity of radio in the 1930s and 1940s put an end to traveling shows of all kinds, not just magic. Vaudeville disappeared, as did the small dance halls and auditoriums that featured science displays and lectures. Magic as an art form was hurt the most, because audiences couldn't listen to magic tricks on the radio. They could listen to bands and singers and actors and actresses, but magic was something that had to be seen in order to work for an audience.

Magicians had only a few places left to perform, such as small theaters or nightclubs where the audience was having dinner or drinks. It wasn't much, but it kept many magicians in business. Street performers also started showing up in big cities again. If people weren't getting their magic in big halls, they could at least get it on the streets. Magicians were willing to work for a few dollars on the street rather than starve.

Even the popularity of television in the 1950s and 1960s didn't help. When magicians first performed tricks on TV, people didn't believe that what they were watching was real magic. They thought the TV camera wasn't showing them the whole trick.

Then, out of nowhere, a small town in Nevada started looking for a way to entertain tourists.

It was Las Vegas. The city had been growing steadily since the late 1940s, and by the 1960s was a popular tourist destination. Many visitors went to Las Vegas to enjoy its hot dry weather and to

Las Vegas helped reignite interest in magic during the twentieth century.

play slot machines and card games. When they weren't gambling or hanging by the pool, though, those tourists needed entertainment. Magicians, along with singers, dancers, and comedians, provided the perfect solution. These entertainers could set up in small theaters inside the hotels and perform several shows a night, each lasting about an hour. When the shows were finished, the audience could go back to the card games.

As more people flocked to Las Vegas, everything got bigger, from the hotels and the concerts to the magic shows. Huge stages were constructed at hotels like Caesars Palace, the Stardust, the

Siegfried & Roy with one of their white lions.

Aladdin, and Circus Maximus to put on elaborate magic acts that rivaled the great magic halls of the 1800s. Magic had found a new home.

The first magicians to gain fame in Las Vegas were Siegfried Fischbacher and Roy Horn, better known as Siegfried & Roy. The two were German citizens who met in 1957 while working as crew members on a cruise ship. Siegfried spent his spare time on the boat entertaining people with simple tricks like making birds and rabbits disappear. One day Siegfried asked Roy what he thought of his magic tricks. Roy responded that they would be a lot more interesting if Siegfried could make a cheetah disappear.

Roy wasn't joking; he had a pet cheetah that he kept hidden on board the ship. He offered to help train the animal so Siegfried could use it in his act. The two eventually became partners and traveled around Europe with a magic show that featured animals. Word of their unusual act spread, and in 1967 they were hired to perform in Las Vegas as part of a variety show, the modern-day equivalent of vaudeville. In time, Siegfried & Roy's act became the most popular show in Las Vegas, and perhaps the most famous magic show in the world. The two men even built themselves a huge mansion where they lived with the animals—especially rare white tigers—that were part of their act.

Las Vegas kept getting bigger, and its appetite for magicians kept increasing. Television talk shows of the time, looking for exciting guests and locations, started taping their shows in Las Vegas, sometimes interviewing the magicians about their acts.

By the early 1970s, TV had evolved to the point where it could present magic in the way it deserved. Color television sets added sparkle to the shows that black-and-white TVs couldn't convey. And shows filmed the action close-up so the audience felt more a part of what was happening onstage.

The first magician to take full advantage of color TV, along with the growing popularity of stage magic in Las Vegas and the relatively new appeal of rock and roll, was Doug Henning. A young man from Canada, Henning didn't look anything like magicians who had come before. He had long hair and a mustache and wore rainbow-colored outfits that looked like the clothes rock musicians and hippies wore. Most important, he had a huge smile and a playful attitude.

Henning grew up wanting to be a doctor. During college, he performed magic at parties and restaurants to make money. Word spread about his unique magical abilities, and he was invited to perform at a Christmas show for Canadian soldiers stationed near the North Pole. Henning's show was such a success that in the early 1970s he persuaded the Canadian government to give him money to develop magic as an art form. The government reluctantly agreed, and Henning set about preparing to bring magic back to the theatrical stage.

He bought old stage props and worked with musicians to create *Spellbound*, a theater show that was part rock concert and part magic act. Henning performed classic illusions from the past, including levitation and even sleight of hand tricks. And he wove it all into a dramatic story, much as Maskelyne and Devant had done years before.

The crowds loved it, and in 1974 Henning took the show to

Doug Henning brought playfulness to magic.

Broadway, renaming it *The Magic Show.* The show was nominated for several Tony Awards, and Henning became a sensation.

It wasn't long before the TV business came calling. NBC, one of the largest TV networks, decided the time was right to put magic on the air in a big way, and it chose Henning to be its magician. On the day after Christmas 1975, Henning had his own prime-time special that was broadcast all across the country. During the live show, he made a woman vanish from under a sheet, sawed another woman in half, performed a card trick, and finished up by performing Houdini's Water Torture Cell stunt.

Henning's TV special was a huge success. Overnight, magic was back in the public spotlight, and people wanted more. The NBC network invited him back to perform a new special every year for the next six years.

It seemed like a return to the golden days of magic. Hotels across the country were booking magic acts. And other TV networks were ready to add magic to their prime-time lineups.

TRICK
❋ 7 ❋

THE ZIGZAG TRICK

👉 **THE ZIGZAG TRICK** is similar to the idea of sawing someone in half, except the person is standing up and is cut into several pieces. But it is really more of an optical illusion than anything else.

A person steps into a three-part cabinet, like a small closet. Three separate doors with individual holes are closed on her. The woman's face shows through a hole, as do her hands and one foot.

With a little bit of theatricality, the magician separates the three sections. Most important, the middle section is pushed so far to one side, it appears that the woman's torso has been pushed completely off her legs. This leaves her head and one of her hands sitting in the top box without any body underneath them. To prove that the hands or feet aren't fake, the magician will usually allow people to shake the hands of the woman in the cabinet, or have her take ahold of something he's holding, like a scarf.

When the audience is sufficiently amazed, the magician pushes the sections back together, and out jumps the woman, still holding the scarf.

The secret is that the trick relies on how the box is painted. All three sections are connected by what looks like a narrow vertical beam. But the beam is painted to make it look thinner than it is. Vertical black stripes on the individual boxes appear to represent solid space but are actually providing several more inches of empty space. Additionally, the placement of the holes is designed to make you think the woman is facing forward the entire time.

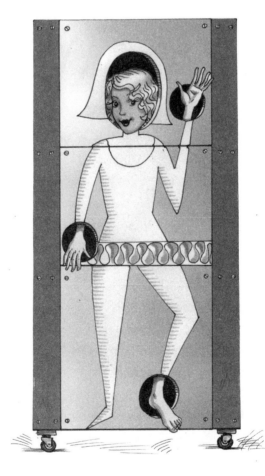

What's really happening is that the woman has turned sideways and scrunched into the narrow space where the beam is. It's a tight fit, but there's more room than your eyes think there is. She's leaning into each of the sections as if she were partially sitting on a stool, angling her body to keep her head, hands, and feet in place. When the trick is over and the three boxes are realigned, she simply twists her body back to make it look as if she'd been standing normally the whole time.

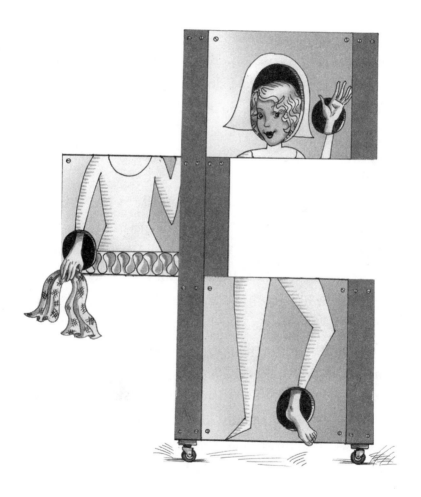

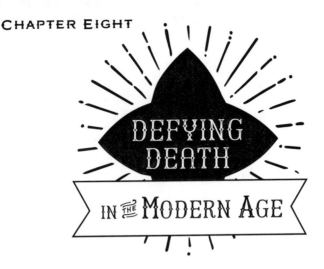

CHAPTER EIGHT

DEFYING DEATH

IN ☰ MODERN AGE

THE POPULARITY OF MAGIC ACTS EXTENDED FAR BEYOND Las Vegas and Broadway. But big magic shows weren't designed to travel; they needed elaborate stages and equipment that weren't easy to move. So people came to see the shows in person, from all around the world. The TV networks realized they could get big audiences to watch those same shows from the comfort of their own homes.

In 1977 the ABC network—which competed with NBC—ran its own magic special featuring a young magician named David Copperfield. Born as David Kotkin in 1956, he became interested in magic as a seven-year-old after his grandfather taught him a card trick. When he began performing magic five years later, Kotkin chose the stage name David Copperfield—the name of the main character in a book written by Charles Dickens.

At the age of twelve, David Copperfield became the youngest person ever admitted to the Society of American Magicians. When he was sixteen, an age when most kids are just learning to drive, Copperfield was teaching a college course in magic at New York University. Copperfield's plan to get his own college education was put on hold when he was asked to be the star of a musical called *The Magic Man*, which was being staged in Chicago. As part of the show, he performed illusions, sang, and danced. He was like all the parts of a vaudeville show in one performer.

Copperfield's TV special was called *The Magic of ABC, Starring David Copperfield*. It literally made the young magician famous in just a few hours. It was so successful that ABC decided to showcase a new set of Copperfield's tricks every year. Copperfield realized that with millions of people watching him, he

David Copperfield has created elaborate illusions specifically for television.

couldn't do the kinds of illusions most people had seen or heard about. He knew he had to create spectacles that would make people's jaws drop. Thinking back to Houdini's Vanishing Elephant Trick, Copperfield decided to go big . . . really big. For his 1981 special, Copperfield chose to make a jet airplane disappear in front of the cameras.

The jet was lit up by spotlights and then surrounded by a human chain—dozens of people who held hands and circled the plane. They were blindfolded to make sure they couldn't see how the trick was done, and they were told not to break the chain. Copperfield then had a huge screen placed in front of the plane and dramatically turned out the spotlights. When he flipped the lights back on a few seconds later, the screen was pulled down and the plane was gone . . . but the blindfolded people were still holding hands. Like the Vanishing Elephant, people are still wondering how he did it.

Over the next few years, Copperfield created several eye-popping illusions. He made the Statue of Liberty disappear, he walked through the Great Wall of China, and he levitated over the Grand Canyon. Thanks to television, these shows were seen by millions of people. Each show was witnessed by more people than had ever seen Houdini in all his shows combined.

Copperfield spent an average of two years preparing for each of his big events, and his levitation over the Grand Canyon was said to have taken five years to get just right.

When he wasn't doing his TV specials, Copperfield was touring the world with his stage act. By the early twenty-first century—a hundred years after Houdini was at the height of his fame—Copperfield was one of the richest entertainers in the world. He created a secret museum in Las Vegas where he currently stores thousands of props that have been used in many of the world's greatest tricks, including automata made by Robert-Houdin and Houdini's Water Torture Cell. Copperfield allows only certain magicians and researchers to visit the museum. He is determined that some magic secrets will always remain secret. True to that ideal, even the exact location of the museum is a secret.

With TV and Las Vegas showing magic acts nearly every hour

of the day and night, magicians were once again entertainers with as much celebrity as singers and actors and actresses. Magic's new popularity allowed magicians with very different styles to create acts that ranged from the simple to spectacular, and from the humorous to the horrific.

While Siegfried & Roy and David Copperfield were creating huge spectacles on giant stages in large theaters in the 1990s, other magicians were finding a way to put their own personal spins on magic.

One of the most well-known acts to have turned traditional magic upside down is Penn & Teller, two performers who have combined magic with comedy. Penn Jillette is a large, boisterous

The duo of Penn & Teller mix wit, sly humor, and even the secrets behind their tricks into their act.

TOOLS OF THE TRADE: LIGHT

Lighting is extraordinarily important to magic that is performed on an indoor stage. Not only do spotlights focus our attention on one part of the action—while something secretive is going on across the stage—they also help the magician distract us. When you think about it, magic is all about fooling the eye. It's not about fooling your ears or nose or tongue. And your eyes rely on light to take in details of a scene.

At a magic show, there is usually a spotlight focused on one part of the stage where the magician is, or there are a lot of lights flashing as if the stage were part of a rock concert. Flashing lights make us unsure of where to look. If they are too bright, they can also make it hard for us to see. Magicians can use a bright flash, such as a small explosion, to make us suddenly look away from one part of a trick. That bright flash might also temporarily make it difficult for us to see anything clearly as our eyes try to readjust back to the darkness.

There are a few modern magicians, like Penn & Teller and Criss Angel, who have broken with tradition and performed some of their stunts outdoors during the day. This adds a riskier element to their acts because it forces them to perform without the kinds of shadows created by spotlights on a dark indoor stage. In their own way, they are toying with an old phrase: they are bringing their tricks "into the open light of day."

Siegfried & Roy effectively use light in their performances.

man with a ponytail who speaks quickly and tells nonstop jokes. His partner, Teller (whose legal name is just Teller, nothing else), is a small man who never speaks a word, yet performs incredible tricks. Penn & Teller are unique in the world of magic because they often show the audience how their tricks are done.

Perhaps their most popular feat is a version of Cups and Balls. Penn & Teller do Cups and Balls with clear plastic cups so the audience can see every part of the trick. They've done the Bullet Catch with each other, firing at the same time. They also slow down some of their tricks so the audience can see how cards or other objects were hidden. They've even done a version of sawing a person in half—although in their version, Teller is put in a box that is then spread out all over the stage . . . and his body parts move in all of them.

This trick is one of those that Penn & Teller reveal to the audience. They do this by removing the front of the stage so that the audience can see what is going on underneath the stage and behind the scenes. They see Teller moving quickly under the stage from one side to the other and sticking his head and hands up in different places to make it appear as if parts of his body are in different places onstage.

Even though they reveal some of their tricks, Penn & Teller are so skilled that it is hard to follow their movements. Even after seeing them perform Cups and Balls with plastic cups, most people could never repeat the trick.

Penn & Teller also take delight, as John Nevil Maskelyne and Harry Houdini once did, in exposing frauds who claim to have supernatural powers. There was a huge interest in the supernatural at the beginning of the twenty-first century. Several TV reality shows featured modern-day spiritualists, people who claimed to talk to the dead. These individuals performed the same tricks that were used at séances hundreds of years before. Penn & Teller created a TV show specifically to demonstrate how spiritualists perform their acts. (No spiritualist in history has ever been able to prove they were doing something other than fooling people.)

Magicians like David Copperfield and Penn & Teller have remained popular to this day. Sadly, Doug Henning died in 2000, and Siegfried & Roy stopped performing after Roy was mauled onstage in 2003 by one of the tigers in their act. Yet the twenty-first century has already produced two extremely popular magicians who not only perform all over the world, but who also have their own TV shows and websites. In the tradition of Houdini, they also perform stunts in public that attract huge amounts of attention, and their expertise is discussed all over the Internet. They are both, coincidentally, from New York, yet their acts are completely different from each other. Their names are Criss Angel and David Blaine.

Criss Angel blends an impressive set of illusions with an attitude and fashion style that is equal parts goth and heavy metal. As a young boy (his birth name is Christopher Sarantakos), he was shown a magic trick by his aunt and then began learning tricks on his own. He dedicated himself to becoming a thoroughly modern magician, even using rock music that he composed in his act. By the time he was twenty, Angel was a popular nightclub entertainer, but he had bigger ambitions. Angel created his own Broadway show called *Mindfreak*, which made him an international

*Criss Angel's stage show combines the spectacle of
a rock concert with traditional magic.*

star. The show featured thundering music, lots of equipment and special effects, a little bit of horror, and some amazing stunts. In a way, he combined the best parts of magicians from the past: the large spectacle of Jean Robert-Houdin, the drama of John Nevil Maskelyne, the scare factor of P. T. Selbit, and the Broadway sensibility of Doug Henning.

Angel took *Mindfreak* to TV, where it became a regular series. Each episode showed Angel preparing for and performing a magic trick, usually a very dangerous trick. In one, he locked himself in a box that was then blown up with dynamite. In another, he hung from a helicopter by fishhooks inserted into his skin.

Many of Angel's tricks are performed outdoors. He does this to show that (maybe) he isn't using all the special equipment stage magicians use. One of his most famous tricks took place in a city park, and it was a horrifying spectacle. He had members of his audience pull on a woman's legs. Suddenly her body ripped in half right below her waist. Unbelievably, her top half then crawled away. This illusion truly shocked his audience, who thought it was seeing something out of a scary movie. (They wouldn't have been so shocked if they had known the woman was chosen especially for the trick. She had lived most of her life without legs and had always walked on her hands. The legs that pulled away from her were fake.)

Angel is also a master of publicity stunts. In 2007 he had himself suspended from a crane above Times Square in New York. It was similar to what Houdini had done in a straitjacket a century before, but Angel wasn't in a straitjacket: he was in a concrete cube. The cube, which was four feet on each side, was hoisted forty feet above the street. Angel was determined to stay in this small box for twenty-four hours while viewers watched him with a webcam mounted inside the cube. After exactly twenty-four hours, the box was released from the crane, and it smashed into the ground below. It probably goes without saying that Angel had found his way out of the concrete coffin just seconds before it fell back to Earth.

While Criss Angel's performances are extravagant and full of flash, David Blaine is all about endurance. In his performances, he sees how long he can survive in a dangerous or difficult situation. His performances resemble Houdini's in that he is usually locked inside an enclosure . . . but unlike Houdini, he is in no hurry to escape. The longer he stays in the enclosure, the better.

ENDURANCE ARTISTS

Throughout history, hundreds of people have claimed to have magical powers that allowed their bodies to do things other people could not. The truth is, these people were not doing anything magical at all. They had trained their bodies over a very long period of time to get used to dealing with things that would kill the rest of us, or at least make us very sick. Here's a list of the kinds of things people have claimed the magical power to do:

- stone eating
- stone swallowing
- knife swallowing
- poison eating
- poison resisting
- holding molten lead or hot oil
- walking into blacksmith furnaces
- squeezing into small boxes
- shrinking themselves
- growing themselves
- fire eating
- glass eating
- metal eating
- "anything" eating (mostly live animals like snakes and fish)
- body piercing
- burning

There were numerous ways to accomplish these unappetizing feats. For example, a person who ate fire was used to having his or her mouth burned and blistered. Over time, he or she had either gotten used to the pain or there was enough scar tissue in that person's mouth that the fire didn't bother him or her too much. Some performers coated parts of their body with pastes or ointments to prevent the fire or poison from actually touching their skin. Albertus Magnus (the builder of the talking brass head in the 1200s) reportedly wrote of a way to actually hold fire by first coating the hand with a fire-resistant mixture made from water, beans, and buttercups.

Occasionally, the people who did these feats were physically abnormal. They were contortionists or were unable to feel extreme levels of pain. Some died from performing these acts, which goes to prove they weren't simple magic tricks.

There are still a number of performers who subject themselves to dangerous tests of endurance, and their stunts are accompanied with the types of publicity that would have impressed Houdini.

Born in 1973, Blaine began his career as a street performer in New York, amazing small crowds with variations on card and coin tricks. He took an entirely different approach than stage magicians: he performed in a T-shirt and jeans, and he presented his tricks without much flash or flair. He projected an air of calm as if his tricks were the most natural and normal things in the world.

In 1999 he began doing stunts that were less about Sleight of Hand and more about survival. He created events that tested the physical limits of his body. His first stunt was to be buried underground in a clear plastic coffin. To ensure he couldn't dig himself out, the coffin was placed under a tank filled with three tons of water. People could walk up to the water tank and look down to see Blaine in the coffin below. News cameras and passersby watched him day and night for a week. He stayed for seven days without food. Finally, weak but alive, he was removed from the coffin.

Many of his stunts have been performed in New York City in full view of anybody who wandered by. In 2000, he was encased in a block of ice for sixty-three hours in Times Square just outside the *Good Morning America* studios (not far from where Criss Angel would later spend his twenty-four hours in a concrete cube). In 2002, Blaine stood on a ninety-foot-tall pole in the park behind the New York Public Library for a day and a half. He also lived in a glass cage hanging from the bottom of a London bridge for one month without food or water. In 2008, he held his breath for more than seventeen minutes on *The Oprah Winfrey Show*.

Many people have taken to calling Blaine an endurance artist instead of a magician, but there is no doubt that his stunts attract attention in the same way that Houdini's did. Houdini's own niece, a woman named Marie Blood, actually went to watch Blaine in the plastic coffin and was said to be very impressed. Blaine claims his performances aren't magic tricks but real feats of human daring and danger.

David Blaine has gained fame as a present-day endurance artist.

TRICK ✷8✷

THE TOOTHPICK TRICK

WHILE CRISS ANGEL AND DAVID BLAINE are known for doing daredevil stunts as well as magic, they are both adept at things like Sleight of Hand. This is commonly referred to as street magic or party magic and is designed to be done very quickly with very little preparation. One of the tricks Angel has shared with his audiences is this very simple Disappearing Toothpick Trick.

Take a toothpick and place a small strip of Scotch tape, about half an inch long, horizontally across the end of it. Tape the toothpick, with the long end sticking down, to your left thumbnail. Wiggle the toothpick around to create some space, like a small cylinder in the tape, and then remove it from the tape. Now the tape is stuck to your thumb as a holder for the toothpick.

Pick up a toothpick from wherever you've placed it (a table, a box, your teeth) with your right hand and put it into your left hand, making it look as if you're grabbing it with your left index finger and thumb. What you've really done is insert the toothpick into the tape cylinder so that the end is sticking up, and the index finger isn't holding anything. Your index finger's main purpose is to look as if it's supporting the toothpick, and to cover the Scotch tape.

On the count of three, splay your fingers wide open and the toothpick will disappear.

What happened was that the toothpick simply laid down behind your thumb, still attached by the Scotch tape. Make sure you keep your palms facing forward so no one can see the toothpick behind your thumb. To make the toothpick reappear out of nowhere, wave your hand and fold your thumb so the toothpick stands up. Quickly, bring your index finger around so it looks like the toothpick magically reappeared between your thumb and forefinger.

EPILOGUE

AGIC HAS CERTAINLY COME A LONG WAY SINCE THE DAYS of Cups and Balls. It has detoured through witch hunts and sideshows, through the labs of alchemists to the early days of television, from the street corner to the Broadway stage.

Magic has survived because tricks have made their way secretly from generation to generation, always creating a new group of magicians that thrill their audiences. Some of these magicians are known all over the world, like Harry Houdini and David Copperfield, while others, like Professor Pinetti and Charles Morritt, are barely remembered.

But it is neither fame nor fortune that makes a magician great. We don't really care if they are known all over the world or just in our town. Because there is only one thing that matters to us when it comes to magic, and it is this: we want magicians to make us believe, if only for a little while, that the impossible is really quite possible.

AUTHOR'S NOTE

I'M WELL AWARE THAT A BOOK ON MAGIC IS REALLY NOT QUITE complete, or quite as much fun, unless I share with you some of the secrets that are used in magic. I'm not supposed to tell you how the tricks are done, because part of keeping magic alive is not revealing the secrets. But you've come quite far in this book, so I think you deserve to get some "inside information" about magic. I won't give you all the answers—there are plenty of magic shops and websites that will give you those—but I can prepare you to start seeing magic for what it is: very clever tricks performed by very clever people.

Here are a few things that will help you figure out, on your own, how magic tricks are done:

- Nothing ever happens by accident in a magic show. Ever. Everything is always planned (unless the trick fails).

- A "normal deck of cards" is usually not a normal deck of cards. It has special markings, as well as duplicate cards, that make a trick work.

- There are more things going on under a stage and backstage than there are on the stage.

- Mirrors are one of the best tools for fooling an audience. A very clean mirror, angled just the right way, will make you think you're seeing through something when you're actually seeing a reflection of something else.

- Thin black thread is practically invisible from a distance.

- Magicians work hard and prepare for years to become good at a trick. They also spend hours before every performance getting ready. If a magician says he is using an "ordinary, everyday" something, he has probably worked on it for a very long time to make it "unordinary." That may mean coating a newspaper with varnish to make it waterproof, or putting clear sticky tape on the back of his hands, or adding extra pockets to a jacket.

- Springs, gears, machines, invisible thread, wires, and fake body parts are all part of the magician's bag of tricks.

- A two-foot-tall wire birdcage can be flattened to just over an inch high and pop up to its regular height with the right kind of springs.

- There is usually something up a magician's sleeve. And also in his or her coat, shirt, and all the pockets.

- Optical illusions are very important for tricks. The way a stage is decorated or the way lines are painted often fool your brain into thinking something is different than it really is. A good example is the use of perspective in the design of a stage.

- Mind readers are good at one thing, but it is not reading minds. What they are really good at is using code words. Good code words can tell a blindfolded assistant what a magician is holding in his hands. For instance, if I say, "I now hold something in my fingers," that could be the code that I'm holding a cell phone. By changing the words slightly to "In front of me, I am now holding something," it could be the code that means I'm actually holding a book. Mind readers have great memories—there are lots of code words to memorize—but they can't read another person's thoughts.

- Magicians say one thing to make you think something else, or to convince you that a trick is completely random. My favorite is called the force. Let's say a magician has hidden a coin inside one orange out of three. He wants to perform a trick that looks like you've picked a random orange . . . and eventually he'll want to pull the coin out of that random orange.

We'll call the oranges A, B, and C. Orange C has the coin in it. The magician wants to make sure you pick C and not the others because the final part of the trick will be peeling the orange and showing you the coin. He gives the illusion of randomness by asking you to pick any one of the three. If you pick C, he says, "Okay, you picked this one, so we'll use this for the trick." He has the right orange in his hand and gets rid of the other two.

If you pick A, though, he says, "That's great, that's the first one to go. Now there are two left; which one do you want?" If you pick B, then he says, "Okay, we'll also get rid of that one, which leaves us with just this one, Orange C. So we'll use C." He has forced you to pick the correct orange without your knowing it.

Now you know what to look for the next time you watch a magician.

—HP NEWQUIST

RESEARCH AND RECOMMENDATIONS

SUGGESTED READING

The history of magic is one that goes back as far as recorded history itself. Because that history is so very long, I've only been able to touch on a few of the magicians who have amazed audiences over the centuries. There are many more magicians who are worth seeking out because of their influence on magic. These masters include Harry Kellar, Max Malini, Blackstone, The Amazing Kreskin, Mark Wilson, Lance Burton, The Amazing Randi, Philippe Petit, and Ricky Jay. To find out more, check out books and websites dedicated to these astounding performers.

Even though magic has always been a mysterious world of secrets, you can easily find many of those secrets. For writing about the history of magic, I found the following books and websites to be very helpful:

The Discoverie of Witchcraft
Reginald Scot
Original copy, 1584
The New York Public Library

An 1886 reprint of the book can be found at
openlibrary.org/books/OL23295621M/The_discoverie_of_witchcraft

A Conjurer's Confessions
Jean Robert-Houdin
Paris, 1906
An online e-book of Robert-Houdin's book can be found here:
gaslight.mtroyal.ca/houdin.htm

The Unmasking of Robert-Houdin
Harry Houdini
The Publishers Printing Co., 1908
Available as e-book from
archive.org/details/unmaskingrobert00houdgoog

Panorama of Magic
Milbourne Christopher
Dover Publications, 1962
Christopher was a magician, a writer, and a historian who created the
first illustrated history of the art of magic.

Mark Wilson's Complete Course in Magic
Mark Anthony Wilson
Running Press, 2003
One of the best and most complete books on magic, this book takes
readers from easy tricks to advanced performances. Wilson was a very
popular magician in the 1960s and 1970s, and much of his magic is tar-
geted to kids.

Hiding the Elephant: How Magicians Invented the Impossible and Learned to Disappear
Jim Steinmeyer
Da Capo Press, 2004
This book reads almost like a detective story as it searches for the secret to Houdini's greatest trick.

Tesla: Master of Lightning
The web home of the PBS documentary, it explores Tesla's life and his inventions.
pbs.org/tesla/ll/ll_whoradio.html

To learn more about the tricks themselves, and the ways to perform them, the Internet has hundreds of sites that do everything from teaching magic to selling props. Here are some of the best:

MagicTricks.com
This site has minibiographies of many magicians as well as lists of tricks, inventors, grave sites, magic works, and fascinating trivia. Visitors can also buy tricks here:
magictricks.com/library/

Classic Magic
This site presents visitors with articles on how to perform a variety of tricks from the simple to the complicated, including sleight of hand and coin tricks.
classicmagic.net/

How to Do Magic Tricks

A site that reveals the secrets to some old-fashioned tricks.

wikihow.com/do-magic-tricks

Metacafe Magic Tricks

Metacafe and youtube.com are online resources where people post videos on how to do a wide number of things, including magic tricks. Check with your parents before logging on.

metacafe.com/topics/magic_tricks/

ACKNOWLEDGMENTS

N O BOOK IS EVER CREATED BY MAGIC. HOWEVER, IT TOOK A great deal of sleight of hand to get this particular book to see the light of day. From the moment I thought up the idea of writing about the history of magic, people around me worked their sorcery to make it a reality. They include Ken Wright, whose ability to find a home for the book was no illusion; Alec Shane, who kept the stage lights on; Kate Waters, who did the initial editing and wielded more wizardry with her pen than anyone could do with a wand; Amy Allen and Julia Sooy, whose prestidigitation shaped it all into something presentable; and the team at Henry Holt, who conjured up the book you have in front of you.

I am grateful to the Rare Book Division of the New York Public Library and librarian Kyle Triplett for granting me access to an original 1584 copy of Reginald Scot's *The Discoverie of Witchcraft*. History is an amazing thing, especially when it's four hundred years old and you can hold it in your hand.

A thanks to those who have supported me since the days when a laptop computer would have been considered witchcraft: my parents, who bought me my first typewriter—and the occasional magic book—in the seemingly medieval times of my youth; my brothers and sisters and their families, especially my nieces and nephews, all of whom bring their own stage show to the party whenever we get together. The mesmerizing friends and supporters I've had over the years: Michael and Barb Johnson and family, Tucker Greco (RIP) and family, Bill Brahos, Bill Leary, Peter Fitzpatrick, Bill McGuinness, Al Mowrer, Philip Chapnick, David Hill, and writing cohorts Pete Prown and Rich Maloof. As always, a wave of the wand and a tip of the hat to the teachers who encouraged me decades ago: John Kunkel and Thomas Werge.

Several people performed the dangerous feat of housing me on the road while I was writing this book: Deb and Dave Shlager, Jim and Margot Shinnick, Rod and Christine Hansen, and Waverly and Bud Henderson. A heartfelt round of applause to you all for your inescapable hospitality.

From under the spotlights, thanks to Peter Koppes and Steve Kilbey of The Church, whose song "The Disillusionist" provided the soundtrack to the writing of this book. Kilbey's lyrics ("He can turn wine into water, mother against daughter / And he does the Indian rope trick, the one that makes you seasick / some of it's done with mirrors and some of it's done with scissors / It doesn't matter, you want to believe . . .") perfectly capture the mysterious and haunting nature of magic—whether it comes from the stage or other realms.

And finally, my eternal gratitude to the three women who add magic to my life each and every day: Trini, Madeline, and Katherine.

INDEX

The Lord of the Rings, 8

Magic Cabinet, 58–59
The Magic Man, 119
The Magic of ABC, Starring David Copperfield, 119
The Magic Show (Henning), 112–13
magic societies, 102–3, 118
magic theater. *See* stage magic
magical powers, 10–11
magical words, 14–15, 90
The Magician (Bosch), 12–13
magicians
  Buchinger as, 26–28
  Copperfield as, 55, 118–21, 125
  Devant as, 86–87
  Henning as, 112–14, 125–26
  Houdini as, 30, 55, 68–84
  Maskelyne as, 57, 62–64, 86, 95, 124
  Morritt as, 50, 83, 85–86, 98
  Pinetti as, 35–39
  Robert-Houdin as, 42–44, 46–47, 51, 53–54, 68–69
  Selbit as, 95, 98–101, 126
  Siegfried & Roy as, 110–11, 121, 125
  Tesla as, 91–95
  Thurston as, 87–88
magician-scientist. *See also* alchemists
  Pinetti as, 35–39
  Tesla as, 91–95
magnets, 45–47
Magnus, Albertus, 33, 129
Marabouts of Algeria, 47
Marconi, Guglielmo, 94
Maskelyne, John Nevil, 124
  levitation by, 63–64, 86, 95
  spiritualists tricks revealed by, 57, 62–63
  tradition of, 126
mechanical lifts, 65–67
Memoirs of Robert-Houdin, Ambassador, Author and Conjurer (Robert-Houdin), 68
mentalism, 46, 48–50, 68
mentalist, xi
  Morritt as, 50, 83
  Robert-Houdin as, 46, 68
Merlin, 8–9
Merry Devil, 96
microscopes, 28
Milk Can Escape, 77–79
Mindfreak (Angel), 125–26
mirrors, ix, 55, 58–62, 83, 137

Morritt, Charles
  as illusionist, 85–86, 98
  as mentalist, 50, 83
  most dangerous trick. *See* Bullet Catch
  musicals, with magic. *See The Magic Man*
mythical origins, 3

NBC television, 114
New York City, 68–69
  Angel stunts in, 127
  Blaine performance in, 130–31
  Henning in, 112, 114
  Houdini in, 81–83
  Statue of Liberty disappearing in, 120
  Tesla in, 93–94
  vaudeville in, 69–71

oddest escape. *See* dead sea monster trick
oldest trick. *See* Cups and Balls
oracles, 7
outdoor performance, 119–20, 122–23, 127, 130–31

peace ray, 94
Penn & Teller, 121, 124–25
performance clothing
  of Angel, 125
  of Henning, 112
  as nobleman, 36
  of pointed hats and robes, 9
  of Robert-Houdin, 44
performance places, 27–28, 62–64
  on Broadway, 112, 125–26
  in grand castle halls, 24
  at indoor theaters, 40–41, 81–82, 86–87
  in Las Vegas, 109–11
  in outdoors, 119–20, 122–23, 127, 130–31
  at public gatherings, 23
  in road shows, 24–25
  in vaudeville shows, 69–71
physics, 29
Pinetti, Giuseppe, 35
  Buchinger compared to, 38
  London performance of, 37–39
  performing as professor, 36
popularity, 108–9
potions and spells, 8–9, 23
prestidigitation. *See* sleight of hand
priests, 7–8
props, 55–56

animals as, 26, 52, 79, 85–86, 88, 110–11, 125
  of cups and balls, 16–19, 124
  of electric chair, 96
  of handcuffs, 74–76
  of professor Pinetti, 36–37
  secret museum of, 120
  straitjackets as, 77, 80–81
  women as, 98–101, 114

Queen of England, 87

rabbit trick, 52
Rahner, Wilhelmina Beatrice "Bess," 72–73
religious beliefs, 10, 20–21
reputation
  as cheats, liars and thieves, 12
  as friend of the devil, 10
  as witches, 9, 11–12, 20–23
Ringling Bros. Barnum & Bailey Circus, 42
rings, 11
Robert-Houdin, Jean
  autobiography of, 68–69
  as automata maker, 42–44
  Light and Heavy Chest performance of, 44, 46
  as national hero, 47
  Second Sight performance of, 46
  secrets of, 51, 53–54
  tradition of, 126
ropes, 89–90

Sammonicus, Quintus Serenus, 14
San Francisco, 74–75
Sarantakos, Christopher. *See* Angel, Criss
Sawing Through a Woman, 98–101, 114
science, 25, 28–29
  automata in, 32–35, 38, 42–44, 104–5
  early understandings and, 20, 23–24, 28
  of electricity, 91–97
  magic of, performing, 35–39, 91–94
Scot, Reginald, 21–22, 68
Scotland, 51
Second Sight, 46, 48–50, 68
secrets
  copycats of, 62
  of cutting a person in half, 98–101, 104–7, 114, 124

INDEX

HP NEWQUIST

is the author of more than twenty books for both children and adults, including *The Book of Blood* and *Here There Be Monsters.* He spends his time exploring the world and writing about everything from music to magic.

NEWQUISTBOOKS.COM

MAGICIANS NEVER REVEAL THEIR SECRETS....

BUT HP NEWQUIST LIFTS THE VEIL IN THIS ILLUSTRATED HISTORY OF MAGIC.

MAGIC is a word we use to describe something amazing awe-inspiring, or spectacular. Truly great magic makes us believ what we know can't be real—be it a death-defying escape or a sim ple sleight of hand.

HP Newquist explains how the world's most famous trick were created, unlocking the secrets behind centuries of magi and illusion, from the oracles of ancient Egypt and the wizards o medieval Europe to the exploits of Houdini and modern practi tioners such as Criss Angel and Penn & Teller. With illustration and step-by-step instructions for eight classic magic tricks, thi book is sure to keep readers spellbound.

> "Strikes a good balance between the history and practical magic tricks.... An enthralling read."
> —CHILDREN'S LITERATURE

> "Fledgling magicians will be spellbound."
> —BOOKLIST

> "This offering stands out from similar books because of the amount of material it provides about various conjurers, illusionists, and mind readers. Newquist does not hesitate to give away trade secrets."
> —SCHOOL LIBRARY JOURNAL

AGES 9–13

US $12.99 / CAN $17.99
ISBN 978-1-250-11539-3

51299

9 781250 115393

SQUARE FISH
NEW YORK ∎ MACKIDS.COM

KAREN TEI YAMASHITA

LETTERS TO MEMORY